EMBRACING OUR PLACE

Strategies, Struggles, and Successes of Ministry Wives

Compiled by the
General Ministers' Wives Fellowship Board
of the IPHC

Edited by Faye Leggett, Director

CONTENTS

Successes

Acknowledgments

To the Ministers' Wives Fellowship Board: Virginia Duncan, Nan Carpenter, Freda Wood, Susan Beacham, Faye Hedgepeth, Imogene Fowler, Michelle Drake, and Faye Leggett, for the vision to have this book written and published.

To all the contributors, who did beautiful jobs sharing their various perspectives. Thank you for your willingness to share your time and yourselves with us.

To Sylvia Long, who planned to write a chapter but, due to a lengthy illness and her recent death, could not. Her invaluable insight will be missed.

To Kimberly Wilkerson, for doing such a wonderful job editing and compiling this book into its current form. Without her, we could never have come up with this finished product.

To all those who prayed, encouraged, and cheered us on in this much-needed task.

And, finally, **to all the ministers' wives**. You are the inspiration for this labor of love. We salute you.

Foreword

To introduce you to this book is to open a window into the heart of the Ministers' Wives Fellowship Board. Our overwhelming desire was to furnish a book for ministers' wives that would help meet so many of the needs and concerns they face in their public and private lives.

In these pages, you will hear the heart of other ministry wives, women who have experienced the very same things so many of you are facing right now. You may feel alone in your circumstance, facing a situation no one else can understand. Take heart. Hopefully, this book will lift you up and draw you into the fellowship of your sisters in ministry who share both your struggles and successes.

As we put this manuscript together, I wished more than once that this information had been available years ago. What a difference it would have made to draw from the experiences and insights of others instead of struggling to find out the answers on our own, feeling all the while as if we were different because we experienced these things!

Each of you is a unique vessel designed by our Creator. You have different personalities but so often face the same situations, hurts, and fears. Many of you have similar wounds, but we hope you find in the pages of this book healing, encouragement, strength, and strategies to *embrace your place* beside your husband.

This book cherishes the uniqueness of women who support their men in ministry. Each of the contributors, although different in so many ways, belongs to a select group of people described in Hebrews 11:38 as persons "of whom the world [is] not worthy."

We believe God entrusted you with opportunities to impact the nation, renew the hearts of the churches you minister in, and lead your children and grandchildren to Christ. Through this book, it is our intent to empower and affirm you. You are important to God, the church, and your families. We salute you.

Contributors

Sharon Atkinson is the wife of Tony Atkinson, superintendent of Ephesians 4 Network and pastor of Celebration Center in Belpre, Ohio. Sharon works at the church, in addition to serving as MWF director for Ephesians 4 Network. Years as ministry wife: 28.

Susan Beacham is the wife of Doug Beacham, current executive director of Church Education Ministries. She is the director of pharmacy, laboratory services, and respiratory therapy at Oklahoma Heart Hospital in Oklahoma City. Susan is also a member of the Ministers' Wives Fellowship board. Years as ministry wife: 33.

Dayna Belcher is the wife of Curtis Belcher, superintendent of the Golden West Conference. She and her husband copastor The Carpenter's House in Fontana, California. Years as ministry wife: 25.

Mary Burchett is the wife of Dwight Burchett, pastor of Life Christian Center in Oklahoma City for 40 years. Now retired from full-time pastoring, Mary enjoys speaking and has a great sense of humor. Years as ministry wife: 42.

Hope Carpenter, a well-known speaker, is the wife of Ron Carpenter, Jr. They are the pastors and cofounders of Redemption World Outreach Center in Greenville, South Carolina, a church with over 7,000 members. Years as ministry wife: 15.

Michelle Drake is the wife of Randell Drake, current superintendent of New Horizons Ministries. She is a first-grade teacher and also serves as the New Horizons MWF director. Michelle is also a member of the Ministers' Wives Fellowship board. Years as ministry wife: 23.

Fay Hedgepeth is the wife of John Hedgepeth, pastor of Northwood Temple in Fayetteville, North Carolina, for 37 years. She is assistant principal of Northwood Temple Academy. Fay is also a member of the Ministers' Wives Fellowship board. Years as ministry wife: 41.

Emily Wood Jackson is the wife of Ryan Jackson. Previously on staff at Northwood Temple, they now reside in Germany and will soon move to England, where Ryan will continue his studies at Oxford University. Emily is the daughter of Edward and Freda Wood. Years as ministry wife: 3.

Faye Leggett is the wife of Bishop James Leggett, General Superintendent of the IPHC. She currently serves as director of Ministers' Wives Fellowship for the denomination. Years as ministry wife: 44.

Thelma McDowell is the wife of James McDowell, superintendent of the Heartland Conference. She is executive secretary to Ron Carpenter, Sr., and also directs WIN and MWF for the Heartland Conference. Years as ministry wife: 41.

Doris Moore is the wife of Ronald Moore, superintendent of the Upper South Carolina Conference. She served eight years as director of IPHC Women's Ministries. Years as ministry wife: 46.

Judith Phelps is the wife of Maurice Phelps, pastor of the PH Church in Morehead City, North Carolina, for 20 years. Years as ministry wife: 35.

Melba Potter is the widow of Mark Potter, who served as superintendent of the South Carolina Conference at the time of his death. Years as ministry wife: 36.

Jewelle Stewart is the wife of Rabon Stewart. Together, they have served as pastors, church planters, and conference superintendent. Jewelle currently serves as executive director of Women's Ministries for the IPHC. Years as ministry wife: 44.

Margaret Stone is a pseudonym. She and her husband have served in various ministry capacities over the years, including pastor, church planter, missionary, and conference leadership. They continue to have a powerful impact around the world.

STRATEGIES

- ***The Real Me, Stand Up***

- ***Life to the Full***

- ***Juggling Act***

- ***Surviving Transitions***

- ***Let's Talk About Mentoring***

- ***Kwik Kourse on Kash Kontrol***

- ***Necessary***

The Real Me, Stand Up

Authenticity in Ministry

by Sharon Atkinson

Seated on the front row of *most* churches is a lonely woman who wears a protective mask to hide her true identity. She is the "First Lady" of her congregation, the pastor's wife. Expected to play the piano, teach Sunday school, be the perfect hostess, sing in the choir, care for her husband, raise flawless children, and set an example of outward beauty and inward spiritual maturity, is it any wonder she is hesitant to remove her mask, possibly to reveal a less than perfect person?

As pastors' wives, we can all identify with the woman in the '60s song who "wears a mask that she keeps in a jar by the door." We've become experts at wearing the ministry mask to avoid the risk of being seen as we really are – less than perfect. We've become so accustomed to wearing our disguises that eventually we hardly recognize our own selves. The façade says to others, "I'm fine; I'm always happy; my house is in order; I have it together, and my children even rise up and call me blessed." Yeah, right! It's time we get real and face the fact that God truly knows us and did not call us into ministry because we were perfect. He was seeking someone real and genuine, a willing vessel through whom He could touch the world. God was far more interested in our authenticity than in our perfection!

Like every other pastor's wife, I have questioned God's purpose in choosing me for this honored position beside my husband. He knew my faults and weaknesses, and yet He led me to marry a man called to ministry ... what was He thinking?

As a student attending Emmanuel College, I remember telling my dad, "I will *never* marry a preacher!" God must surely have laughed out loud at my proclamation while simultaneously directing my steps to meet the man of my dreams, my future husband ... a man He had called to ministry!

Having grown up in Franklin Springs, Georgia, the former IPHC headquarters, I had the privilege of knowing many godly women who held the title of pastor's wife. In fact, I lived next door to my own pastor's wife, Glenda Swails, the epitome of grace, beauty, and godliness. How in the world could God expect me to keep company with such perfect women? At all times, Mrs. Swails was pleasant and loving and consistently wore a beautiful smile. (I do believe she smiled in her sleep.) Even working in her yard, she was appropriately dressed and never appeared to sweat ... she simply glistened. I was terrified at the thought of being expected to fill the shoes of such a seemingly perfect woman. For goodness' sake, I actually sweat!

As I grew older, however, I began to recognize a common factor among particular women, like my own pastor's wife, who made lasting impressions on the lives of others. Those who were most effective in ministry and exhibited consistent joy were the women who were genuine and authentic. They did not "put on airs" nor pretend to be someone else. They were real ... the same both in public and in private. These women had found their identity in Jesus Christ, not in a title or in their profession. They were real and genuine examples that others were drawn to follow and emulate. Because of their authenticity, these women made a positive impact on the lives of those who looked to them for leadership.

After 28 years of ministry and much time spent with pastors' wives, it has become quite evident that I am not the only woman who has wrestled with the fear of being the "real me" and possibly failing to measure up to the expectations of ministry. Our highly visible lives seem to require us to *be* and *do* more than other women. No other profession puts more pressure to meet expectations on the shoulders of the spouse.

Someone once said, "A pastor's wife is the only woman who is asked to work full time without pay on her husband's job in a role no one has yet defined!" Can I hear two amens and a hallelujah? Because of these pressures and expectations, many pastors' wives are unwilling to reveal their true identities at the risk of rejection or failure.

I believe four major identity robbers attempt to steal our authenticity in this honorable yet sometimes difficult role of ministry. Yielding to their pressure will rob us of our freshness, originality, and true potential in ministry. These robbers are **approval seeking**, **unrealistic expectations**, **fear of intimidation**, and **comparison with others**.

Approval seeking. People-pleasing is not only futile, but unscriptural. Galatians 1:10 tells us that we are to be God-pleasers, not man-pleasers. Because it is not possible to please everyone, seeking people's approval will always leave us with feelings of failure and inadequacy. If you are a natural people-pleaser, ministry will kill you unless you learn to look to Jesus for your approval and affirmation. Your effectiveness as a leader will be greatly hindered if your pursuit of man's approval is the focus of your attention. Oswald Chambers wrote, "If I am devoted to the cause of humanity only, I will soon be exhausted and come to the place where my love for God will falter, but if I love Jesus Christ personally and passionately, I can serve humanity though people treat me like a doormat." What excellent advice to us as pastors' wives. We can risk being real because it is not people we seek to impress, but God we desire to please no matter how others treat us. Written in the cover of my Bible I have a powerful confession reminding me that my highest priority in ministry is to please God. *"I will live my life in pursuit of God's purpose for me. My self worth is not determined by the opinion of others, and it is to God that I will ultimately answer for my life. For this reason, I will live, first and foremost, to please God."*

Unrealistic expectations. Recalling our early years of ministry, I remember my frantic attempt to meet every expectation placed on me to please our congregation and to be the perfect helpmate to my husband. Together, we juggled the responsibilities of the church. I cleaned the restrooms while Tony mowed the grass; I played the piano while he led the singing; I taught children's church (with baby on hip), cooked for church dinners, visited the sick, comforted the lonely, prayed for the needy, and was kind to the grumpy. Needless to say, I was one thoroughly exhausted and mean woman. (I am convinced that the only difference between a pit bull and an overworked pastor's wife is lipstick!) Yes, ministry is spelled W-O-R-K, but it is not our responsibility as pastors' wives to do it all. Life is so much easier, joyful, and rewarding when we learn to respond to realistic expectations, operate within our own gift mix, and simply be what God called us to be ... *real!*

Pastors' wives often deal with the pressure of "performing the expected." Our identity becomes confused with *what we do* instead of *who we are.* Burnout is the ultimate result of placing our priority of "doing" over that of "being." Being real involves honesty with ourselves and with others instead of yielding to the pressure of unrealistic expectations. We must recognize the limits of our personal giftings and release the remaining responsibilities to qualified people around us. We must ask ourselves, "Do I do the things I do because it is expected of me or because God has gifted me to do them?"

Fear of intimidation. We are told in Deuteronomy 1:17 not to be afraid of any man because judgment belongs to God. The fear of intimidation causes us to experience feelings of inferiority and inadequacy. When these things threaten our confidence, we must remind ourselves that promotion comes from God, and it was He, not man, who placed us in the role of pastor's wife. It is very important to remember that no one can make you feel inferior without your consent. Often, we allow others to close the door on God's destiny for our lives for no reason other than the fear of the face of man.

Comparison with others. The "comparison trap" is one of the most common tools of the enemy to hinder women from operating in their God-given abilities. We were created to be as

4

different and individual as every snowflake falling on a winter's day. Why, then, do we try so hard to be carbon copies of those around us? We must embrace the gifts and personalities God has given us. God wants to use *you* to influence others. He is looking for authentic examples for people to follow, not identical ones. I have learned that when I use the gifts I *do* have to their fullest potential, people don't look for the ones I *don't* have! When we are tempted to compare ourselves with others, we must remember that God designed each of us specifically to *fit* her own husband, church, and calling. We must be ourselves and use the gifts God has given us. If you won't be yourself, who will?

One of the best ways for a pastor's wife to minister to the women in her church is to be *real*. Be the best you can be, but be *yourself*. We face the same struggles as those to whom we minister, and God never intended us to be fake. His destiny for your life is that you minister with your own unique personality and giftings to those people He has placed around you. The best example we can be is one that is authentic. Your church will never know your true potential until you stand up and be the *real* you.

For years, I struggled with very common identity issues among most pastors' wives ... feelings of unworthiness and inadequacy. What a freedom I experienced when God showed me that it is not *my* ability, goodness, or worthiness that makes me qualified for ministry, but *God's* ability in me. Suddenly, it wasn't so difficult for the real Sharon to stand up. The pressure was off. I could be myself, living to please God while setting the best example I can for others.

> ***Prayer Point:*** *Lord, remind me that you called me for who I am. My life should be about seeking your approval, not the approval of others.*

I came to understand that God does not choose leaders based on natural talent, ability, age, or experience. Timothy's youth and Moses' lack of experience were proof of this. God chooses leaders based on their availability, and He qualifies those He calls! He simply wants me to be myself, to the best of my ability, and allow Him to do the rest!

This understanding opened a new door of freedom for me to utilize gifts I had hidden long ago, fearing they would be inappropriate or unacceptable. I realized, for instance, that my sense of humor was actually "God-given," and He expected me to use it to minister to people He had placed around me. Guess what! It really is okay to laugh and *enjoy* this Christian life. You see, God equips those He calls in the manner He chooses. Never believe that your gifts and talents are not suitable. What an encouragement it was for me to find in 1 Corinthians 1:26-31 that God has chosen to manifest His power through *the foolish and the weak!* I realized He, too, has a sense of humor, and there really is hope for me. Never underestimate the gifts in your life ... God will use you if you will just step out and be yourself.

Being real allows others to see your humanity. People cannot follow a perfect example; they long for a *real* one! Being real keeps us on the same level with those to whom we are called to minister. The highest compliments I receive in ministry have been those from people who thank me for being real. Although it is easier to hide behind the ministry mask, I find that I am unable to reach people when I try to make them think I'm perfect. Being a real, genuine, and authentic example of God's grace ministers far more effectively than attempting to be someone I am not. It's all right for others to see me cry, to hear me laugh, to know I hurt, to hear me admit my mistakes and to ask their forgiveness. When the burden of "performance perfection" fell from my shoulders, I experienced a whole new level of ministry to others ... a much deeper level that allowed me to genuinely touch the lives of others. In other words, my influence is most effective when I allow the real Sharon to stand up. Imagine that!

It was humbling to discover that the basis of my hesitancy to reveal my true self was nothing more than a fear of being

6

embarrassed before others. Basically, it was pride that kept me from being real ... a fear that my imperfections would be uncovered. I look back with much regret at missed opportunities to minister to the needs of others because I was so absorbed in my pursuit of perfection. We cannot afford to live our lives behind the false mask of prideful perfection. People need to see that we, as leaders, look to God for our ability to be and do all we are in ministry, just as we teach them to do. Laying down your "perfection mask" will be the best decision you ever make. People simply need the real you, warts and all, to exemplify an authentic life genuinely lived for God.

> **Prayer Point:** *Ask God to help you remove the mask you hide behind every day. Expose your true self to the light of His love. Bask in the glow of His approval and acceptance. Reveal the real you to those you serve in the church.*

Through the years, I have also experienced the pain of betrayal from those I have allowed to see me as I really am. We have all been hurt by those who have used our weaknesses, failures, and shortcomings against us. With this in mind, I am ever mindful that boundaries to our realness in ministry are imperative. Being real with others does not mean we let down our guard. There is wisdom to be used in our level of transparency. Jesus was real with people, but Scripture tells us He "did not entrust Himself to them because He knew the nature of mankind" (John 2:24). Airing our faults and failures with sheer abandon leads to a dangerous familiarity with others that will hinder our ability to lead them. Remember: God forgets; people do not. God's Word says that a righteous man is cautious in friendship (Proverbs 12:26). As pastors' wives, it is important that we be "real" but that we also use caution in the degree to which we become transparent.

"What is expected of me?" is the most common question I am asked by pastors' wives. My response has become,

"Be yourself, be real, and be genuine." People are looking for someone who will listen to their needs, love them unconditionally, and teach them, by example, to live a life that pleases God. Simply be authentic!

As pastors' wives, we should be who we are, not because of our title, but first and foremost because we are Christian women. Our identity is not based on the amount of work we do or the opinion, approval, or expectations of others. Who we are should be founded simply in the fact that we are children of God.

It is vital that a pastor's wife understand and operate in her God-given identity. How will she help other women understand their full potential if she has not discovered the freedom of doing the same? It has been said that we cannot lead others beyond the place we ourselves have gone. The pastor's wife who is most effective in her influence is one who has found her true identity in Christ Jesus. She knows her rights and stands her ground, is not timid or fearful, and though she does her best, does not pretend to be perfect.

It is not your own strength, ability, or righteousness that makes you who you are, but Christ *in* you. It has taken me years of struggling with my identity to rest finally in the knowledge that I am who I am, and I can do what I do *only* because God has placed His hand on my life. Being real is recognizing that He will equip me for every task required of my calling, and in His strength I can do all things.

It would be dishonest to say at this point in my life that I no longer care what others think of me, but I can truthfully say that I no longer have anything to prove. I am me. God created me with my own unique personality, gifts, and abilities suited for the purpose of ministering to those He has placed around me.

We must remember that we were handpicked even before our birth. God planned our destiny long before we ever accepted Him. He was fully aware of our weaknesses and strengths when He made His choice. We may not be all we desire to be at this moment, but be assured that God is faithful to equip those He calls, and with His help, we can be all He planned for us to be. Until then, we must remove our masks and be real women who trust God to do all He promised in our lives.

There is no limit to what God can do through you if you will only find your identity in Him. God can use you just as you are. You don't have to pretend to be more spiritual or more gifted than you really are. God wants you to be real and authentic, yielding your life as a vessel He can use to influence many with your own unique style. We are all called to be authentic, not false or copied but genuine, real, and trustworthy women. It is my prayer that you will ask God for the courage to "stand up and be the real you." There is such freedom in being yourself!

Sitting on the front row of *some* churches is a happy and contented woman who is real and free to be herself. She knows her limits and does not yield to unrealistic expectations. Her identity is found in Christ Jesus and not in the opinion of others. Using her own gifts to the best of her ability, she does not compare herself to others, nor is she intimidated by their talents. Others may see her cry, hear her laugh, feel her hurt, and witness her failures. Although not perfect, her life is one lived in genuine pursuit of the things of God and sets an example others are eager to follow. She is the First Lady of her church; she is real; she is authentic; *she is the pastor's wife.*

> **Prayer Point:** *God, help me above all to take off my mask in the presence of my husband. Teach me to minister beside him in the freedom of your grace.*

Life to the Full

My Family Is My Ministry

by Doris Moore

Everyone wants a life that matters. John 10:10 says that God also wants our lives to have real meaning and value: "I came to give life and life to the full." But as women, wives, mothers, professionals, and ministry partners, the journey for this kind of life can be a difficult road to traverse.

When my husband and I married, we knew from the beginning that we were destined for a life in "the ministry." For us, this often meant full-time pastoring with part-time pay. My husband served as an associate pastor while we both worked full-time jobs. Our first son arrived shortly after our first anniversary. At this time, my husband felt we were to pioneer a church in his home state of South Carolina. For those who know anything about church-planting, this means full-time work with no pay! We both continued working our jobs while building a strong community of believers. That's when son number two arrived. This was a time of hard work and sweet memories as we were beginning our new life together, building our ministry, and quickly adding to our family. After a few years, my husband was offered the pastorate of a small but thriving church. So we, a family of four, made the move and shortly became a family of five. The journey was now getting interesting.

At this time, in 1968, my husband and I decided that he should return to college for further education. This meant that I would need to go back to work full-time. Yes, we were still pastoring, and yes, we still had three boys – under the age of 8!

At the time, we simply did what we had to do and followed the Lord's direction. It is only now that the thought comes to my mind, "What on earth was I thinking?"

During these times of juggling work and school schedules, day-care, church meetings and activities, and family time, I had to do some real soul-searching. What exactly was my purpose in life? I loved being a wife and mother, I loved teaching school, and I loved the church work, but how could I do it all and do it all well? I needed to know my purpose. Proverbs says that "without vision the people perish." Looking back, if I hadn't gotten a vision for my life, marriage, and family, we, or at least my sanity, might have perished!

My vision and purpose came as I began to establish priorities for myself. These priorities did not change any of the circumstances, but they did give me perspective and purpose. I am so grateful for how the heavenly Father graciously guides our thoughts and our steps as we remain connected and obedient to Him. As I sought the Lord about who He wanted me to be and what He wanted me to do, I began to get a vision for my life and our family. I began to understand how vital my role was as wife and mother and that my most important "job" was purposefully to set the spirit of our home. I also soon realized that the way I went about this was crucial.

> **Prayer Point:** *Ask God to invade every layer of your life and reveal the areas which are essential (priorities) and those that are nonessential. His wisdom is available to help you establish vision and purpose for your life and your home.*

In order to set the right spirit in our home, I had to set the right spirit in my own heart and life. This was possible only through a sincere and vibrant relationship with our Lord Jesus Christ. I realized that the key to ministry to my family was to realize that God is the head of the home, and my first priority had to be my personal relationship with Him. Everything else in life flows from this relationship with God. When we begin to speak, believe, and act upon Joshua 1:9 – "As for me and my house, we will serve the Lord" – God will honor our desires to see our family loving and serving Him.

We all face the challenge of establishing priorities with everything in life – to diet or eat that extra helping of pecan pie, to buy that sparkling new car or drive the "beater" for another year. But some priorities have much more serious consequences than others. Putting God first and foremost must be the primary goal of every individual.

Family rather than ministry should be next in our line of priorities. Ministry to my family has always been easy for me because I feel that of all the blessings God has given me, my family is the greatest. I am grateful for the gracious opportunity of having a loving husband and three of the most wonderful sons in the world. God has truly blessed me as a wife and mother. While I have enjoyed many other areas of ministry, my greatest has been and continues to be ministry to my family.

A healthy home is the result of healthy relationships. It begins with a loving relationship between husband and wife. Once children come along, somehow we can begin to overlook our spouses and get busy with many other people and things. We must remember that as women, our second priority is our relationship with our husbands. Remember that you were a family even before the children came along, and you will continue to be even after the children leave home. I had to remind myself *not* to neglect my wonderful husband and to remember that we need each other. A healthy marriage is one of the best gifts we can give our children. When they see this model played out before them, it will have a positive influence on their relationships with each other and those outside the home.

> **Prayer Point:** God, grant my husband and me the continuing grace to live and love together as a testimony to your glory.

This does not mean that marriage and family life are always easy. Living in a minister's home is not always a bed of roses. It has often been referred to as "living in a glass house." You can be sure that raising three boys in a parsonage was quite a challenge. There was always someone ready to point out the mischief of three active boys. And believe you me, there were many mischievous deeds – leaping across the hoods of parked cars during service, making prank phone calls, and the list could go on! One thing that helped me tremendously in this area was always to listen carefully to the complaints, but not to make any decisions regarding the crime and punishment until I heard the boys' accounts. Then the appropriate consequences were privately administered. God has given us the responsibility of training our children, and He holds us accountable for the way we raise them. I appreciated the concern of the church family, but I had to keep in mind always that I was responsible ultimately to God for the training of our boys, and not to the "concerned others."

I remember when the boys were quite young, we took them to the circus. We did not tell the boys to keep our family outing a secret, so naturally, the youngest had to share the excitement of such an adventure. The news that the pastor and his wife had taken their children to the circus was not smiled upon by one of the church leaders. He privately reprimanded us for this action. We listened and then politely communicated that we saw no harm in going to the circus, and we knew that we must give an account to God for what we allowed our boys to do. He apologized, and all was forgiven. I am glad that early on, we learned that we do not and cannot please everyone, so the key is to focus on pleasing God and answering to Him.

This is also true in the area of discipline. It seemed that in our home, this was one subject that was addressed daily! It seemed that one of the boys needed some type of discipline every time we turned around. In fact, discipline was given so often that we devised a plan to help them in this matter, which also helped us retain our own sanity. We put a chalkboard beside the telephone and kept the boys' names on it. When one got into trouble, he had to put a mark beside his name, and when he got three marks, it was time for the paddle. It was amazing how much this helped in their discipline.

It was important for us as parents to understand what type of discipline worked best for each child. Talking was all that was needed with one, while another didn't understand anything but a good paddling. Whatever forms the discipline takes, however, it must always be covered with love. I never understood as a child when my mother told me that it hurt her more than it did me when she would discipline me. Only when I became a mother did I understand the truth of that statement. It hurts to see your child disobey to the point that firm discipline is needed, but it is a necessary part of child-rearing. We learned that it is crucial in this process to be consistent and honest. Don't correct for a wrong one time and then allow that same wrong to be overlooked at another time. Don't tell them one thing and then do the very opposite. Say what you mean, and carry through with your words. This modeling of honesty will teach children that to be honest is one of the greatest attributes a person can possess.

The real key in setting the spirit in our homes and with our children is to concentrate on their hearts even more than their outward actions. Understanding the nature of your child will help you in the development of his or her character. Children are not always able to communicate their true feelings, thoughts, and motives, so we must continually be sensitive to what they are trying to get across and the reasons behind their actions. Help them to understand that God has a place for them in His kingdom, and His plan is always best. It is easy for us as parents to develop a plan for our children's lives, but it is much better to train and lead them to understand and follow God's will for their lives. This means that we have to give our children room to fail and then a helping hand to help them overcome that failure. It is not always wise to fix every problem that arises. Sometimes we have to let them work through the problem, but always be there for them with hope and encouragement when they need them.

> **Prayer Point:** *God, I need insight and wisdom to rear my children as empowered believers. Give me eyes to see their hearts, and ears to hear their inner longings.*

I am thankful that our boys learned early how to seek God for His will in their lives. We taught them to seek God for the answers in all things and to carry through with what He directed for them. This has become very evident as we have watched our sons grow and develop into their exciting areas of ministry. All three of them are in ministry today and enjoying the blessings of God. There is no greater joy that can come to parents than to know their children are walking in obedience to the will of God in His chosen ministry for each of them.

Healthy Relationships

Throughout my journey, I have found three important elements necessary for healthy relationships, whether with God, spouse, or children. One is the *value of forgiveness*. Forgiveness must be willingly given when it is asked for, and even at times when it is not. Demonstrating this principle is so much more effective than just telling them. Don't be afraid to say, "I'm sorry" or "I was wrong." When a child sees a parent ask for forgiveness, he or she will be more apt to follow that example when forgiveness is needed in his or her life. It is important for us as parents to remember that our self-worth is not based on the behavior of our children. It does not tag us as a good or bad parent, but it does give us an opportunity continually to demonstrate God's love and forgiveness. Proverbs tells us to "train up a child in the way he should go, and when he is old, he will not depart from it."

The second element is found in the three words that cannot be repeated too often: *"I love you."* When I have a conversation with our children, even now that they are grown and married with children of their own, I try never to end without saying, "I love you." It is important in the development of the balanced life of a child to hear those words. I truly believe that our children will remember these words when they are tempted to stray from home, believe a lie, or take a wrong turn. Knowing that they are dearly loved can have an important bearing on their lives. Our boys had a wonderful example of this in their father, who constantly told them that he loved them and also told me that he loved me. I am grateful for how he taught our boys to love and respect their mother. Today, I watch them as they carry this same teaching to their own children, as they love and respect their wives.

The third vital element of a healthy relationship is perhaps the greatest gift we can give. It is *the gift of prayer*. Nothing is more powerful or valuable than to cover our husbands and children daily with prayer. Satan often attacks us in the weakest areas of our lives, and often that is our relationships. If he can attack our husbands or children, then he has attacked us. Pray a wall of protection around them as they leave for the office, for school, to visit a parishioner or friend, or anytime they walk out of the house. Ask God to protect them and bring them safely home. Let them hear you praying for them. They will never get away from those prayers. I can still remember hearing my mother calling my name in a prayer of protection as I was leaving the house or at night while I was in bed.

As a young minister's wife, I pledged to love and support my husband in the work into which God called him. It has not been without struggles, but the joys have been much greater than the heartaches. Watching our three boys grow to be mighty men of God has been a source of joy that comes only from a life of commitment to God and family. I feel they are three of my greatest contributions to the kingdom of God. We were taught in our early years of training that the church was our most important ministry, that ministry to our family always followed. I am glad we did not accept this teaching. Even when my husband and I were overwhelmed with ministry to the church, it was our ministry to our family that became our primary personal challenge. Ministry to my husband and our boys became and continues to be my life, as I pour into the lives of our wonderful grandchildren. I am thankful that I found my purpose and that God equipped me with wisdom, patience, and a loving heart to trust Him for my family.

God established the home before He established the church. He tells us to look well to the needs of our households. I believe that when we do this, all other ministry will follow. As women, we have been given an awesome privilege and responsibility to stand beside our husbands and to nurture our children in the fear of the Lord. Motherhood is one of the greatest gifts we can receive and use to further the kingdom of God. Now, that is what I call "life to the full"!

> ***Prayer Point:*** *Ask God for a mentor to guide you as you "look well to the needs of your household." He is a loving Father, more than willing to grant your request.*

Juggling Act

Realities of the Working Pastor's Wife

by Susan Beacham

For two years, almost every Sunday morning began with my driving an hour to work. After ensuring all work areas were functioning properly, I would drive back home, get the children ready for church, practice with the organist during Sunday school, play for the worship service, jump back in the car, and drive another hour back to work while listening to my husband's sermon on radio. And he thought he had a busy Sunday!

The last 20 years of our married life has been in one form or another a juggling act of working mom, wife, and pastor's wife, with all the expectations, joys, and frustrations that each brings. I've learned some things over these years that may help you deal with the issues that come with this package.

Every pastor's wife is at least bivocational. That is, we take care of home, children, and husband, as well as serve the Lord in some capacity in the local congregation. Regardless of our role in the church, we balance two interrelated worlds that impact our homes and the ministry. This is the given situation for every pastor's wife, whether she works outside the home or not.

The Trivocational Reality

Did the opening story resonate with any of you? Perhaps you're the schoolteacher who hurries home on Wednesday night for Missionettes, or you're a nurse trying desperately to trade schedules with someone so you can be at church on Easter

Sunday, or you're working long hours in a retail store. We know what it means to be "bivocational." What does "trivocational" mean?

Trivocational means that besides our responsibilities to our families and local congregations, we also have responsibilities in the workplace. With the added time pressures, why do we do this?

First, many do this because we feel called to help support the family so our husbands can give full-time or at least more time to the ministry of the local church. We may feel frustrated because the local church is not yet able to provide adequate compensation for our husbands. We then feel guilty about feeling that way! This is a common scenario for wives involved in church planting as well as in churches experiencing revitalization.

Second, sometimes we have had to work because of financial struggles. We wanted to be fully involved in our husband's ministry. We dreamed of "team ministry" and discovered that either poor financial decisions or circumstances beyond our control (such as a serious illness) forced us into the marketplace.

Third, perhaps you and your husband have made financial decisions based on your mutual priorities that demand a two-income family. For instance, you decided to enroll your children in private school, and it is necessary for you to work outside the home to accomplish this family goal.

Fourth, many of us are called to serve Christ in a workplace environment. We see this as part of our ministry. This added sphere of our ministry does not relieve us from the added stress of family and congregational demands and expectations.

Regardless of your particular circumstances, you understand the particular stress points and opportunities that arise from being a "trivocational" pastor's wife.

How Do We Cope?

Previously, we described four common working pastor's wife scenarios. There are elements common as well as distinct to each.

You work so your husband can give more time to the church. Rather than feeling guilty, this is actually part of your calling, at least for this season, as a "helpmate" to your husband. I have heard women say that they feel God is disappointed in them because they cannot give more time to the church. I have good news for you: God is not disappointed in you! You are doing exactly what the Father calls for as a faithful Christian wife to your husband.

Resentment at this situation can become a spiritual wound that infects your heart and ultimately your ministry in the church. We have to be careful that our resentment is not manifested in passive-aggressive behavior or destructive comments about the church and its lay leadership. This is especially true if you think there are people who could do more financially but do not.

> *Prayer Point: First, ask the Holy Spirit to affirm you in what you are doing for your husband and the kingdom of God. Second, ask the Holy Spirit to reveal any wounds that need His cleansing and healing grace in your heart. Third, be thankful for the opportunities you have.*

You work because of financial struggles or setbacks. If you are working because of poor financial decisions in the past or present, then your work situation is a symptom of a deeper spiritual and maturity issue. This requires confession, repentance, and Christian discipline in order to correct. This is more than your personal problem; it is also an issue between you and your husband that affects the whole family. The good news is that God forgives and will provide you with strategies to help you manage your finances. The International Pentecostal Holiness Church has partnered with Crown Financial Ministries to help couples better manage their personal financial resources. You can contact your conference office to find out more about making this ministry available to you and your local church.

Prayer Point: *First, confession and repentance. More than likely, this will involve you and your husband. Second, your prayer is not that God will perform a miracle and rescue you instantly, but that God will give wisdom and discipline in the financial matters of your life. Most of our financial problems occur because we spend not only on our needs but also on our wants. Unfortunately, we easily confuse the two! Our cry needs to be, "Lord, change my 'wanter'!" Third, remember there is no condemnation for those who are in Christ Jesus. The evil one may want to remind you of financial mistakes. God graciously offers forgiveness and give you wisdom if you will ask Him (James 1:5).*

There are other financial setbacks that we did not personally cause, such as illness or an unexpected loss of church income. Again, Crown Financial Ministries is a resource to help you manage during this crisis and recovery. The book of Job is a great spiritual help in this situation. I am encouraged by the story of Job. Job had no knowledge of the exchange between God and Satan and how God allowed the trials to come to him. But God had faith in Job. God has faith in you!

Prayer Point: *Ask God for more patience, trust, strategies, and peace as you walk through this season of life.*

You and your husband have made financial decisions based on your mutual priorities that demand a two-income family. The real issue here is not the financial decision but the priorities you believe are foremost in your family. Each family and each community is different. This is not always a case of "keeping up with the Joneses." There may be very legitimate reasons why your family has decided upon the priorities that are driving your employment decision.

A related issue is to recognize that the seasons may change as certain priorities are fulfilled. For example, private school for elementary school may be a necessity. Private school in later years may be a luxury. This requires great wisdom and a prayerful and candid relationship between you and your spouse. A valuable warning for all of us: we easily become dependent upon that second income, and our lifestyle expenses usually rise in proportion to that income.

> ***Prayer Point:*** *Keep your heart pure, and make certain your priorities are in accordance with God's priorities in this decision.*

You are called to serve Christ in a workplace environment. We see this as part of our ministry. We feel as "called" to this as our husbands feel "called" to the church. However, I firmly believe that my job should never supersede God's call upon my husband's ministry. If God is calling him to relocate, then I believe God has a place for me to serve Him in that new location. With wise planning, this second income becomes a conduit for God's greater purposes through both of you.

This does not exclude or excuse us from having a ministry in the local church. We have spiritual gifts that can be exercised in both environments. Lois Evans, wife of Anthony Evans of the popular radio ministry *The Urban Alternative*, found her role in ministry in an unusual way. She could not play the piano or sing, the kinds of roles often associated with being a pastor's wife. But she was gifted in business. When the ministry expanded to the point where the church started *The Urban Alternative*, her husband and the church recognized her gift of administration and hired her to oversee the production and expansion of this vital ministry.

> ***Prayer Point:*** *Learn to balance the fulfillment we receive in our jobs with the fulfillment we have in our families and in the local congregation. I have learned to pray Romans 12:1 as paraphrased in The MESSAGE: "So here's what I want you to do, God helping you: Take your everyday, ordinary life – your sleeping, eating,*

going-to-work, and walking-around life – and place it
before God as an offering. Embracing what God does for
you is the best thing you can do for Him."

How Do We Minister?

You may wish you didn't have to work outside the home, or
you may be thrilled with your career. Regardless, as disciples of
Jesus Christ, we must be available to the still, small voice of the
Holy Spirit to seize every opportunity. Romans 12:2 instructs
us, *"Don't become so well-adjusted to your culture that you fit into it*
without even thinking. Instead, fix your attention on God. You'll be
changed from the inside out. Readily recognize what He wants from
you, and quickly respond to it" (The MESSAGE).

With this in mind, there are two questions: 1) How do we
recognize ministry opportunities on the job? and 2) How do we
keep our ears open to hear the voice of God at our jobs?

To illustrate the first, I remember this episode from the
hospital: I received a call from Dr. William Walker requesting
to meet with me. You need to understand that he was quite
volatile, to the point that the staff called him "Wild Bill." I
asked where he was and said I would go to him, but he insisted
on seeing me in my office. I sat there anticipating an unpleasant
and difficult encounter.

You cannot imagine my surprise when "Wild Bill" came
in, closed the door, and with tears in his eyes said, "Tell me
everything you know about the Holy Spirit."

After picking my jaw up from the floor, I asked him, "What
has happened? Why do you want to know?"

He explained that he had recently become a Christian and
was hungry to know more about Christ. During the following
months, we chatted from time to time, and I gave him several
books to read about the Christian life, including Bishop B. E.
Underwood's *The Gifts of the Spirit: Ministries and Manifestations.*

Several years passed, and Bishop Underwood moved to
Franklin Springs, Georgia. Shortly after moving, he was notified

of a suspicious area on his lung from an x-ray taken in Virginia. Since he did not have a local physician, he called me and asked whom I would recommend. I told him that I would recommend Dr. Walker and offered to talk with him about seeing Bishop Underwood.

I called Dr. Walker and explained that I had a friend who needed to be seen. He asked the friend's name, and I told him, "Bishop Bernard Underwood." Dr. Walker immediately exclaimed, "He's the person who wrote the book on the gifts of the Spirit! Tell him to be in my office at 10 a.m." By the way, Dr. Walker is a pulmonologist. I will never forget seeing Dr. Walker pray for Bishop Underwood during their times together! It is awe-inspiring and humbling to realize how God can use what appear to be isolated incidents in our lives to make the way for meeting the needs of someone else.

For some, keeping our ears open at work comes very naturally. Sometimes the Holy Spirit may instruct us to pray quietly for those around us, to offer a word of encouragement, or to "claim the land" where our feet step for His kingdom to be established.

However, He may interrupt the routine of work to shake us from the routine of our Christian life. Let me tell you about an episode that occurred at work that completely changed my life.

It was the week after Christmas in 1997. As a hospital pharmacy manager, I had prepared a research document for a medical staff committee but could not find a functioning copy machine. Finally, I found one that worked in the medical records department. By the way, do I believe that God "broke" the copy machines? Absolutely! It was to get me to the place where I could hear Him speak. I am constantly amazed at the lengths to which God will go to get our attention.

While the copy machine hummed, I began to read the Christmas cards taped to the wall. One immediately captured my attention. It was from a female physician, with whom I had worked, who had recently moved to Quebec, where she and her family were learning French as they prepared for the mission field. In the card, she thanked the department for the monetary support they were sending. After thanking them, she signed the card, "In the name of the One Who is most precious to me, my Jesus."

When I read that line, the Holy Spirit spoke: "Susan, I'm not precious to you."

I started to argue with Him, "I'm a pastor's wife; I play the piano at church; I do..."

He stopped me, and, in a way I can never explain, let me see not only what I did but also my motives. I realized that I was substituting "doing" for an intimate relationship with Him. I did not feel condemnation but an indescribable love. In that instant, I knew the Holy Spirit was right on target. I started crying because I realized that Jesus really was not precious to me. Weeping, I stopped the copy machine and hurried to my office.

To me, one of the miracles of this encounter is that He allowed me to go from the first floor of the hospital to my office on the fifth floor without seeing anyone and having to explain why I was crying. After I was in the office, I put my head on my desk and told the Lord there was one thing I knew about Him: He did not bring me here to leave me like this.

I asked Him, "What do I do?" His answer may surprise you. He told me to go home and tell Doug what had happened. He also gave me specific instructions regarding what I was to do after asking Doug to pray for me.

I went home and came into the study where Doug was reading. I told him what had happened and asked him to pray for me. He asked me, "What do you want me to pray?"

I replied, "I want to love His Word because He has shown me that if I will love His Word, I will fall in love with Him."

Doug started to stand to pray for me, but I stopped him. I said, "The Holy Spirit told me that I must kneel in front of you." This was a major step for me. I was a self-sufficient, career-focused, strong-willed woman, and I knew the Lord was using this to bend my knee to His will. Doug prayed that the Lord would give me the desire of my heart. This was the beginning of a precious and continuing journey into the Word of God. The Lord did give me the desire and prayer of my heart.

Putting It Together

We need to remember that the Bible is full of stories of God's calling people while they are at work. Moses and David were tending sheep; Peter, James, and John were tending their nets; Matthew was collecting taxes; and the list continues to this day. He is calling women like you and me, women who, for whatever reason, work in and out of our churches and homes. The important thing is to remember to listen to His voice. If you will listen carefully, I think you will hear Him calling you today!

Surviving Transitions

I married a youth pastor,
and now I'm the conference superintendent's wife!
How did that happen?

by Michelle Drake

*"To everything there is a season, and a time to every
purpose under the heaven."*
Ecclesiastes 3:1-2

Webster defines *survive* as "to live after another or anything else." *Transition* is defined as "passage from one place, state, or topic to another." So my "minister's wife" definition of *surviving transitions* would be, "Do not let one place kill you, so you can go on to another place!"

Our 1982 wedding invitation could have read, "Small town, rural, sometime Baptist girl to marry cosmopolitan, bona fide Pentecostal Holiness youth pastor; fireworks to follow." We definitely were as different as night and day. People who knew us individually questioned this wedding union. Some wondered if I ever spoke, while others wanted to know why I was marrying "such a nice guy." Even my own mother said, "You can't buy that negligée! You know you are marrying a preacher." My soon-to-be husband even had a dear saint come into his office and let him know our union would never last because we were just too different. (I ran into her about four months ago and just had to remind her how long we'd been married.) All I knew was that I had fallen in love with the most dynamic, bigger-than-life man of integrity I'd ever met. I loved all that he was and all that he represented.

29

That's how it all began almost 2½ decades ago. I often marvel at what the Lord has done in abundantly blessing our union, our ministry, our mission, and our purpose. God has taken us to places beyond what we could have imagined at the time. He is truly an awesome God, and I give Him all the praise, honor, and glory!

My husband, Randell, and I have served five churches in ministry positions as varied as Christian Education director, children's pastor, youth pastor, minister of music, associate pastor, and senior pastor. Randell is currently serving as the superintendent of the New Horizons Ministries Conference of the International Pentecostal Holiness Church. With each ministry position Randell has held, my main focus has been to be his encourager and helpmeet, assisting him to be all that God has called him to be and to do. I've always told him, "I'll move anywhere you say we need to go as long as you can look me in the eye and say, 'God told me we need to go there.'" I vividly remember one time my husband said he felt the Lord directing us from South Carolina back to Oklahoma. I told him, "You'd better look me in the eye and say it, because I love my job [administrator of a private Christian school], my ministry, and my life here in South Carolina." Fortunately, God has always given us a spirit of unity when it came time to transition from one place of ministry to another. We usually both reached this spirit of unity within a couple of weeks.

My husband and I are both first-born children. You know the type: determined, opinionated, headstrong, aggressive, leadership-oriented, and in-charge kinds of people. That's us! So for God to bring us into unity on major decisions is a miracle in itself! That's how we always knew the transitions were God guiding our footsteps along the paths He wanted us to travel.

In reflecting upon each ministry transition, either within the local church body or between churches, the Lord always began to speak to our spirits in advance that a change was going to occur. This happened for Randell as well as for me. We never went looking for ministry changes. The Lord always provided the open doors for our ministry transitions. I truly think the secret to knowing the Lord's will is to seek Him in every decision and rely on the peace that only the Holy Spirit can provide, the peace that passes all understanding.

In transitioning between ministry positions, seven key elements will make the transition a success. I fully believe that if we approach each ministry transition focusing on the seven elements, the transition will be nothing less than a success. These elements have proven to be effective in the course of my 24-year, full-time ministry marriage.

Element One: Settle within your heart that God has placed you in a position or a location for a specific purpose and time. Don't allow Satan to come in and plant seeds of doubt. Don't overanalyze. Don't worry. Just stand upon the Word of God and know that He has a plan and a purpose for your life. Seek the adventure in relocating, shifting gears, and getting new starts! My husband and I grew up in families that relocated quite often. I have always believed that God was preparing me for my role as a minister's wife from the moment of my conception to the day I said, "I do" at Abundant Life Temple in Durant, Oklahoma, 24 years ago.

Element Two: Once you have relocated, it is imperative to get your home in order. Focus on getting things unpacked and putting pictures up on the walls. This will give you and your family a sense of security and stability. It's also fun to decorate rooms and see how everything is going to fit within a different home. I've always been amazed at how God actually makes everything fit in specific places. When we are excited about these transitions, our children will be excited as well. When our family relocated three years ago (our sons were 9 and 11 years old), I was amazed at how smoothly my sons transitioned. We had been in our previous ministry location for five years and loved it. My sons were very involved within the community, their schools, and our church. Their adjustment to the relocation was just another awesome way God showed His majestic presence to me.

Element Three: Begin to work within your own ministry giftings. Find your place, and let God use you. Whether you work outside the home or not, find your ministry place within the church. This could be in the form of choir member, children's church leader or helper, office assistant, Sunday school teacher, or any of the variety of ministry positions within the church. The success of this third element is that it must be within your ministry giftings. I have a dear friend who was drafted into teaching an elementary Sunday school class. She dreaded teaching every Sunday. The class didn't grow, and she didn't want the class to grow. The reason she was so unhappy was that this was not her ministry gifting. It is imperative that the congregation see you using your gifts and talents for the Lord.

Element Four: Respect your husband as the head of his ministry position. God has positioned him for a specific purpose. Your job is not to be your husband's boss. I really have to work on this one. (Remember, we're both first-born children.) Now, there are definite times – at home – you may voice more of an opinion and feel you must keep things moving along (concerning family life), but in ministry, it is not your place to influence him. I do not want my husband making church decisions based upon what I think (and believe me, I have a lot of opinions). However, if our husbands ask for our advice, I believe it is our responsibility to give any insight we might have regarding a specific situation. A fine line exists between offering requested advice and telling a husband what to do. The latter does not prove beneficial in the long run. Remember, it is the Lord's place to guide and direct your husband for His ministry.

Prayer Point: God, give me binoculars and brakes: binoculars to see those things I might share with my husband when asked, and brakes to stop me when I want to be the guide for my husband's ministry.

Element Five: We must *always* speak the positive.
Some good inhabits every situation, so look for the good.
A critical spirit will bring only sadness and regret to the
ministry. Yes, I'm one of those who fully believe every cloud
has a silver lining, and if life gives you a bunch of lemons,
you just make lemonade. One of my favorite verses is found
in Philippians 4:8 (NIV): *"Finally, brothers, whatever is true,
whatever is noble, whatever is right, whatever is pure, whatever
is lovely, whatever is admirable – if anything is excellent or
praiseworthy – think about such things. Whatever you have learned
or received or have heard from me, or seen in me – put it into practice.
And the God of peace will be with you."* A friend of mine once
stated, "If you know how to worry, then you have all the
brain mechanisms in place for praise. Worry is the opposite
of praise. Every time you begin to worry or think negatively,
just begin to praise and think positively." I say, let's retrain
our brains to get rid of "stinkin' thinkin'" and turn it around
to the power of positive thinking! If you do this, the negative
complainers (or faultfinders) in the church will soon realize
they cannot hold you captive and get you to join forces with
their complaining. When my husband was the minister of
music, he very politely told the choir that he was the minister
of music, and anyone who had any suggestions or complaints
should discuss them privately with him, not me. It took only a
few times of my saying, "My husband is the minister of music,
and you really need to talk to him about that," for them to
stop trying to bend my ear or get me to use my influence with
him to get their way. This phrase will also work for other
ministry positions.

**Element Six: God is always teaching us something
we will use in the future.** This element has really come to
fruition during the superintendency stage of our ministry. We
have walked through some rather peculiar circumstances over
the past three years that would have blown us away had we
not gone through something similar in our previous ministry
positions. Each ministry opportunity definitely taught us

valuable lessons. At the time of each eye-opening experience, we couldn't understand why God allowed us to witness such things. Now, we look back and say, "That's why God had us there to walk through that." If you can begin to reflect upon what God has previously taught you and see how it is helping you in the present, your ministry level transitions will be easier. I'm so excited because I don't know what our future ministry will hold, but I do know that God is continually preparing me for it. The ministry is an exciting career. Know that God has you where you are for a purpose!

> *Prayer Point:* God, help me to learn and retain those lessons you are teaching me in this place. Give me wisdom to know when to share those lessons with others.

Element Seven: It is imperative to have respect for authority. If you cannot respect those in authority over you in your church setting due to moral failure, unresolved conflict, or vision differences, begin to pray and ask God for specific ministry direction concerning you and your husband. If you feel you cannot remain in a position due to the above issues, resign quietly and move on. It is not your place to split the church or make congregational members choose sides in your personal conflict with authority. The well-being of the church and maintaining unity in the body are more important than your personal feelings and convictions. In four of the five churches we served, the pastor had a moral failure. My husband had to deal personally with these difficult situations more than I did because of his job, but my emotional and spiritual well-being was affected as well. Throughout these times of prayer and seeking God's will for us, my husband and I learned to depend fully and completely upon God for our peace of mind and reassurance of His ministry plan for our lives.

General Guidelines for Each Ministry Position

Wife of youth minister. Enjoy the youth group. Spend time with the youth group. Host events just for the girls. Respect the senior pastor, and respect the parents of the youth group.

Wife of minister of music. Consider being in the choir so you can model proper choir etiquette. Enjoy the choir members. Be on time for rehearsals, and honor your husband's decisions regarding music selections and productions. Respect the decisions of the senior pastor and church board.

Wife of associate pastor. Be a cheerleader for the pastor, the pastor's wife, and the pastor's children. Accept words of wisdom from the pastor's wife. Respect the decisions of the senior pastor and church board.

Wife of senior pastor. Take an interest in the wives of other staff members. Respect the giftings of the women within your church. Consider hosting a Bible study for the deacon's wives where no church business is discussed.

Wife of conference superintendent. Try to attend as many conference events as possible. Always try to attend the Women's Ministries events. Respect the decisions of the superintendent and the conference board. Send or deliver a small gift to the pastor's wife when you visit her church. If you have children living at home, attend a nearby Pentecostal Holiness church so that you and your children can use your ministry gifts and feel connected with a specific body. Traveling with your husband is the best option if you have no children living at home.

The Lord wants us to survive ministry transitions. The following Scripture empowers us to succeed in ministry. Romans 12 states, *"So here's what I want you to do, God helping you: take your everyday, ordinary life – your sleeping, eating, going-to-work, and walking-around life – and place it before God as an offering. Embracing what God does for us is the best thing you can do for him. Don't become so well adjusted to your culture that you fit into it without even thinking. Instead, fix your attention on God. You'll be changed from the inside out. Readily recognize what He wants from you, and quickly respond to it. Unlike the culture around you, always dragging you down to its level of immaturity, God brings the best out of you, develops well-formed maturity in you"* (The MESSAGE). Place your life before God.

> **Prayer:** *Dear Lord, thank you for opening this door for our ministry. Help me to see you in every aspect of my life and in this ministry. Help me to be who you would have me to be, and, Lord, lead, guide, and direct my footsteps. Help me to be the Spirit-filled, God-loving wife you have destined me to be. Let my husband receive only love, support, and encouragement from me. Lord, help me to balance all the responsibilities you have placed in my life, and help me to prioritize each day. Thank you, Lord, for all you have done in my life. Thank you for the things you will teach me. Help me to learn through each experience. Lord, I stand in awe of who you are, what you've done, and what you're going to do. Amen.*

Let's Talk About Mentoring

The Ministers' Wives' Mandate

by Jewelle E. Stewart

I thought he took me to the end of the world, and it was – at least, the end of my world, with all that was familiar and secure. Just a week before, we stood at the altar in front of my father (he equaled God in my mind) and the entire church. Daddy lowered his brow and posed the question: "Will you take this man...?" My "yes" was unwavering, strong enough to be heard outside the front door. Seven days later, we pulled into the little frame parsonage in Montgomery, Alabama – the farthest place I'd ever been. I felt lost.

A new husband, life, and role as "minister's wife," with all the accompanying responsibilities, stared me in the face. How hard could it be? After all, my mom was a preacher's wife. So was her mom and several of her sisters. Ministers and ministers' wives were in the majority at family gatherings. Surely, something of who and what they were had been passed on to me through the gene pool – a form of "minister's wife osmosis," right?

Wrong! Many rude awakenings waited. Like one thrown into the middle of a maze with never-ending twists and turns, I found it difficult at times to know where and when to turn.

Within a couple years of setting out on this new venture, motherhood was added to the mix, along with work in the public sector. Many changes had occurred at such a fast pace that I could hardly keep up. Pressures and stresses accumulated. I came to a place where I questioned my life's worth and my ability to live up to the expectations of others.

The inner turmoil caused me to question my salvation, for surely preachers' wives never experienced such doubts as those that swirled deep within me.

> *Prayer Point: Ask God to grant peace to the turmoil in your soul. Ask the heavenly Father to reassure you of the special place you hold in His heart. Ask for strength to live up to His expectations, not those of the people around you.*

To my thinking, it shouldn't have been so difficult to adjust to this new life and the list of real and imagined expectations. After all, I was the daughter of a preacher, granddaughter of a preacher, et cetera, et cetera ... Why, I could even play the piano and sing a little! I knew how to smile and be pleasant even if my husband and I had argued on the way to church – a major talent, for sure! All the "credentials" were in order, so what was wrong with this picture? Help was needed – but what kind? Seeing a counselor at that time was unheard of, and most certainly not done by ... a preacher's wife!

"I know," I reasoned. "I'll talk with someone ... but with whom?" I was in a quandary. Several states away from familiar support systems, did I dare turn to people I hardly knew? In the 1960s, the pastor or his wife was a good choice to talk with, but that was not an option. My pastor was my husband; my former pastor, my dad. Okay, what about the next pastoral team in line? My former superintendent had recently died, and his wife, who had been a mentor to me and to so many others, was finding a new way herself. Our present superintendent ... he was family too. This was a maze filled with too many preachers too close for comfort! Still, there was a desperate longing to talk to someone. At a particularly stressful time, I looked around for someone who might lend an understanding ear. I was still a relative newcomer to other ministers and their wives and was too far removed to talk with my sisters. "I know," I thought to myself. "I'll find a Catholic church somewhere and talk with the priest. You're supposed to be able to talk openly to him. He won't know me, and besides, he is sworn to secrecy!"

"You can't do that," self argued. "Someone might see you going in or coming out and get the wrong idea."

Need and conflict collided frequently. I needed a friend besides family or women in the congregation: someone like me – a minister's wife. Throughout this period of time, I never did find that special individual. However, God's hand of grace was extended, and new relationships began to form. Godly women and men who spoke the truth in love and modeled Christlikeness under pressure came across our path. Sometimes, there would be boldness to ask questions. Many times, learning came simply through observation. Renewal came slowly but surely. If others saw through the façade, they were kind to this preacher's wife. We made our way through several pastorates and various other roles that were added through the years, hopefully without causing too much damage along the way. Then, I did not know enough nor trust enough to find someone – another minister's wife – in whom to confide. Now, I understand how important it is for every preacher's wife to have another preacher's wife in her life as a mentor and friend.

> ***Prayer Point:*** *Ask God to send a mentor into your life, or to send you into the life of a younger woman who needs the guidance you have to offer. Be willing and obedient.*

The Need for Mentoring

Women in general today are confronting more complex issues than those of previous generations. In addition to facing a more complex life than their predecessors, those who marry preachers often enter that role with little comprehension of the demands on them personally, on their time and energy, and on their marriage. Ministers' wives need the blessing of other ministers' wives in their lives. Ministers' wives can and should be a place of learning for one another. They need to know – up close and personal – women in like situations, beautiful women who, while having experienced the various aspects of ministerial life, have come through with peace in their hearts and lives. Yes, the Bible is our ultimate handbook through which we learn of God and His eternal plan for creation, but I am convinced God designed people to be His "How To" manuals (see 1 Corinthians 4:16 and 2 Corinthians 3:2, 3). We learn from others, and women, especially ministers' wives, need godly role models in all seasons of life. There are no seminaries ("a place where something develops, grows, or is bred") dedicated to turning out qualified ministers' wives. There probably should be. Until then, we need to talk.

A Biblical Mandate

Jesus began his earthly ministry by selecting 12 to be with him in close fellowship. His command to them was, "Follow me" (see Matthew 4:19). He was saying, "Watch me closely. Learn how to live as I live. Become like me." The principle of being an example, of modeling how to live before others, was not something new in Jesus' day. It is woven throughout Scripture.

In his letter to Titus, Paul instructed him to teach the older women to be reverent in the way they lived so they could teach what is good. Older women were to be in a position to teach the younger women so no one would malign the word of God (Titus 2:3-5, NIV). Paul outlined specific areas to which older women needed to give attention so they could give proper direction to younger women. There is a clear mandate in this passage for one with experience to reach out deliberately with the intent of teaching someone less experienced.

Our responsibility to help another grow is quite biblical. The term used to describe this process in recent years is "mentor." Although the word is not found in the Bible, the principle and practice is solid. "Mentor" comes from the classic poem by Homer, the *Odyssey*. It was the name of a friend King Odysseus entrusted with the care of his son while he went off to fight in the Trojan War. This friend trained the king's son just as the father would have. While this is a mythical pagan figure, we can draw from this example.

Today, "mentor" refers to a coach, guide, counselor, or tutor. It describes someone who assists or helps another less experienced or skilled. It may even apply to someone who helps another reach her God-given potential or prepares her to face future challenges. Mentoring, then, is an opportunity to invest oneself in another, to help one another grow.

Ministers' wives live "in a glass bowl," never far from the scrutiny of the congregation. Whether we realize it or not, we are constantly modeling a lifestyle before others. Women in the congregation and in our communities watch and learn from our behavior. A positive, vibrant, faith-building, and praying minister's wife is a tremendous blessing and greatly needed in today's culture. The world has seen more than enough of downtrodden, hard-times-suffering ministers' wives among our ranks. It's time for ministers' wives who are women of faith to rise up and mentor our daughters. The church needs a new generation of daughters prepared to pick up the torch and become bold in the faith and equipped, taking their stand alongside the young men to reach their generation for Christ! We cannot leave our responsibility to the men. One of my favorite quotes is, "Men can teach women, but it takes a woman to model a godly, feminine lifestyle."

Who, Me?

Paula M. Wilder wrote an article entitled "Bring Mentors Out of Their Shells." She lists several misconceptions about mentors, such as "someone who has it all together, someone who memorizes a new Scripture every day, knows everything about the Bible, never messes up ..." Ms. Wilder states,

Many women, especially older ladies, think they are unqualified, unable, and unworthy to mentor because of those misconceptions. Their reluctance is a shock to us leaders, because we've seen qualities in them that would make them terrific in that role:

- visibly living a life for Christ
- continual reliance on God
- openness about weaknesses and failures
- desire to give God glory for successes
- hunger to share with others what the Lord has taught them

Read her list of qualities again. She could be describing you!

Mentoring Traits

Mentoring successfully will depend on various traits we bring into the relationship. Five that I feel are important from the start, apart from prayer, are disciplines that should already be a part of our lives. (Remember, disciplines are developed with time.) Our weaknesses are no excuse for unavailability. One thing I have discovered is that if we fail in any of these, our effectiveness as mentors will be diminished. Let's talk about them. A mentor needs to be:

A good listener (see Galatians 6:2) – To have someone to talk with who really listens is of supreme value. There are young ministers' wives who are desperate for someone to listen to them, even if they don't seem to make sense at first. Listen; just listen to her. It can be the most valuable gift you can offer. Most people listen for a "hook" they can hang a response on. Practice disciplined listening, and get past the surface words. Hear the heart of the matter. Bearing one another's burdens happens when one extends the blessing of listening. Solutions often surface as we provide the gift of listening.

Nonjudgmental (see 1 Corinthians 10:12, 13) – Women know when they are behaving in a less than sanctified way, especially ministers' wives. Being nonjudgmental does not mean condoning sin. It does mean providing a safe haven for the emotionally weary. As our ranks grow, there will be some who have come to the Lord out of the pagan pool, met the loves of their lives, and BANG ... entered the ministry. They will have experienced the joys of salvation and a clean heart, but will be plagued by the "who" and "what" of their past. I remember one couple who approached us for church membership. There was evidence of a lingering struggle on the part of one, but both had been genuinely converted and Spirit-filled. We were torn between following our hearts and following a tradition until the Holy Spirit cleared it up. "Who are you to reject what the Lord has accepted?" He asked. From that time on, we operated in that word. Deliverance will come. Meanwhile, we offer the same love, acceptance, and forgiveness that the Father has extended to us. (By the way, over the years, the Lord used this couple to disciple more people than almost anyone else we have known. He knows what He is doing!)

Trustworthy, able to keep confidences (see Titus 2:5 and 1 Timothy 1:5) – The greatest hindrance to developing a healthy mentoring relationship might hinge on this trait. It is tempting to share a juicy tidbit someone confided in you with another friend, but guard strongly against it. If we are trustworthy, we provide a covering. If not, we uncover the nakedness of a sister before others. Resist the temptation, keep that confidence and covering. Pray daily for the Lord to set a watch on our lips.

Honest and open (see Philippians 1:10, 1 Thessalonians 2:5-12, and 1 Timothy 4:12) – There is a level of vulnerability that comes with mentoring, but it does not mean every dark and intimate secret is shared. Some things are forever kept under the blood and between husband and wife. Yet there is a level of transparency and risk-taking in a mentoring relationship. The one being mentored needs to know that the more experienced minister's wife does not operate at 100 percent all the time.

As you have opportunity, share your stories. Young women need to hear stories from more experienced ministers' wives, and we need to hear theirs. Older women need to let their guard down and let the younger women teach them about realities of today, just as younger women need to hear of the faithfulness of God through the years. Be sincere, real, and honest. It works!

Affirming (see Ephesians 4:29 and 32, 2 Corinthians 13:12, and Ephesians 1:16) – The New Testament is filled with examples of Christians affirming one another. Some women married to ministers do not receive affirmation from their husbands nor from the congregation. I have known a few. Listen, we need to talk about it! This type of action doesn't surprise us when coming from the pagans, but it is abominable when coming from within the Body. Ministers' wives need affirmation from within their own ranks. The Body of Christ will grow when we put aside every smidgen of jealousy or pride and lavish affirmation on one another. The world needs to know that we love one another even as we love our own lives. Paul put it this way: "Greet one another with a holy kiss." The mentoring relationship will be filled with "spiritual holy kisses" – genuine affirmations flowing from the heart of God and edifying our sisters.

Beginning the Process

Look around. In your own fellowship, district, or conference, there may be one or two ministers' wives who catch your attention. Perhaps you prayed with another minister's wife at a retreat or seminar about a particular need. You have an open door for a follow-up. Perhaps you drew someone's name as a prayer partner. There is a wide-open door! Continue to pray and walk through that door. Perhaps you are new in the role of minister's wife and desire friendship with someone who has been a minister's wife longer than you have. Pray for the Holy Spirit to prepare the way and take the initiative. Don't be deterred or discouraged. Keep praying and reaching out. God has the right connection waiting!

At least twice in our ministry, there came into my life women whom I did not like, whom I could not stand to be around, and with whom I certainly did not want to have a relationship. I didn't want to pray about it either! One happened to be a minister's wife, and the other became a minister's wife later. One wanted to hang around and talk after every service. Excuses did not seem to work with her. She was persistent, and I was adamant with the Lord about having her in my life. The other was quite colorful and dramatic. She had the ability to twist your words into an unrecognizable heap. Thank the Lord, they came at different places of ministry! What do you suppose happened? Right! I couldn't run them off, and God didn't remove them. Each did become a true friend over time. (But I still thank God they came at different places!) I learned from both women and, by God's grace, was able to help them a little. Even those with whom we don't click at first may be the ones God has brought into our lives for their and for our own good.

MWF Provides a Connection

One of the most obvious opportunities where the mentoring process can begin is through Ministers' Wives Fellowship. Encourage ministers' wives to read books on mentoring. Study and teach the Titus 2 mandate as it applies to our role and responsibility to our peer group. Talk about the importance of imparting what we have learned with one another. Take advantage of retreats, conferences, camp meetings, and other events to bring ministers' wives together. Provide a setting other than classroom style (i.e., speaker and rows of chairs). Prepare lead questions or conversation starters, and ask several women of various ages to be prepared to initiate conversations from these starters. Others will participate. Set a mental time limit, and help guide conversations to achieve a balance between the serious and lightheartedness. (Remember, ministers' wives can tell a sad story, if given time.) Give opportunity for prayer requests, and ask the women to pray with those who offered requests in an area where they have experienced a measure of victory. Watch your clock. You can't provide enough time for everyone to pray as long as she desires, but you can provide index cards for the exchange of addresses and phone numbers. Encourage everyone to make contact with someone within two weeks.

Although she was not a minister's wife, the young servant girl had the wisdom to speak to her master, Naaman, a word that led to his healing. Esther, another young woman, acted with great prudence and wisdom. A nation was spared. The relationship of Naomi and Ruth began as an older woman to a younger, but later became a time of the younger blessing the older woman. The lineage of Christ was perpetuated. Elizabeth, an older woman, became a mentor to Mary, the mother of Jesus. And the story continues...

Titus 2:3-5 is a charge for ministers' wives today, and mentoring opportunities are constant. The tendency might be to wait until one is older to consider mentoring. Don't let age stop you. Women mature and grow at different paces. One may be 30 and have 20-somethings looking up to her. There is great potential for mentoring this age group, for they are eager to learn all they can about the ministry. Ministers' wives can mentor others in their peer group or reach out to new brides of ministers. Certainly, older women who have developed in their walk with the Lord should accept the responsibility to share their lives through the mentoring process. One may be 80, a widow of a minister, and feel that her time of ministry has passed. Look around. There is much to offer to the one who has just lost her minister husband. At any given age or stage, there are those who can model and those who can learn.

A Time to Let Go

A word to the wise and to those who would be wise: Mentoring is not a lifelong commitment to an individual. The object is to help her mature and mentor others. Begin with that goal in mind. Review your progress from time to time and, at the proper time, release her to soar with your blessings. There will always be a special bond between the mentor and the one mentored, but there will come a time when you must let her go.

Looking back, the blessings are greater than the stresses, by far. In the over 40 years since that Sunday when I confidently spoke those vows, I have a new perspective on the world and my place in it. The number of godly people in our lives has steadily increased. Maturity has come in some areas, but I have not yet arrived. Since this wonderful, mysterious life called the ministry does not come with a "how to" manual, I will always need other women to speak into my life: women involved in ministry, experienced in places I have yet to venture. From them I can draw wisdom and insight, and together, we will "grow up into Him who is the head" (Ephesians 4:15). God is faithful to His plan of operation, and He is faithful to those who are called by His name. That includes saved preachers' wives – Hallelujah!

Resources:

Books and Study Guides
Donna Otto, *Finding a Mentor; Being a Mentor* (Eugene Oregon: Harvest House Publishers), 2001.
Donna Otto, *The Gentle Art of Mentoring* (Eugene Oregon: Harvest House Publishers), 1997.
Vickie Kraft, *Women Mentoring Women* (Chicago, Illinois: Moody Press), 1992.
Henry A. Simon, *Mentoring: A Tool for Ministry* (St. Louis, MO: Concordia Publishing House), 2001.

Articles
Marion Lorence, "mentoring.com" in *Just Between Us* (Brookfield, WI: Telling the Truth Ministries), Summer 2004.
Paula M. Wilder, "Bring Mentors Out of Their Shells" (LifeWay World Wide Web site), July 6, 2004.

Kwick Kourse on Kash Kontrol

Financial Stewardship for Ministry Families

by Thelma McDowell

When my husband graduated from college and just before we left for our first pastorate, he asked three ministers he respected, "What advice would you give someone just entering the pastorate?" He was surprised that all three gave him the same answer. It was a simple one, but something we have never forgotten. Their answer: "Pay your bills and stay out of debt."

We have thought of that often and formed our lives to live accordingly – after all, what good does it do to ask for advice and not follow it?

Your ministry to your church and your community is much more than just sermons preached or neighborhood forays with the Gospel. It includes sermons lived. A pastor's family that doesn't pay its debts brings reproach upon the local church, the Christian community, and the kingdom of God. So make it a habit to pay your bills – and, I might add, pay them on time!

Avoiding debt is one way to maintain and carry out a healthy financial strategy for your family. In this Kwick Kourse on Kash Kontrol, I hope to help you understand God's plan for your family and how you can achieve it.

Three Things God Wants for You

God wants you to have plenty. Philippians 4:19 (TEV) tells us that "with all his abundant wealth through Christ Jesus, my God will supply all your needs." God is our source of supply. God helped me with a dream to understand about His provision.

In this dream, I was in a house with a two-story cathedral ceiling. Boxes filled the room from floor to ceiling, and I knew in my spirit that everything I would ever need or anyone else would ever need was there. I answered a knock on the door, and there stood the president of one of our colleges and his wife. I asked what they needed, and they told me. But when I turned around to get the supplies for them, I could see no boxes in the room. I told them, "I'm sorry, but there is nothing here."

Immediately, there was a check in my spirit, and I was told, "Just reach in by faith and pull out what you need." In response, I reached into the open space. As I did, the exact supplies they asked for came right out of the empty space and into my hands. Immediately, I awoke and felt God saying in my spirit, "I have everything you need. You might not see it when you look for it, but if you will reach out with arms of faith, I will give it to you."

Your part is to believe and reach out to receive. God wants you to have plenty. He has made provision through Jesus Christ for your needs to be met. Please note, I did not say all your wants would be met, but your needs will be met. It has been my observance, however, that most of your wants (if they are in His will) are provided too.

God wants you to have money to give to the poor. When the needs of your household have been met, God wants and expect you to be generous to those less fortunate. Luke 6:38 (NLT) says, "If you give, you will receive. Your gift will return to you in full measure, pressed down, shaken together to make room for more, and running over. Whatever measure you use in giving – large or small – it will be used to measure what is given back to you." 2 Corinthians 9:7-9 indicates that you should not give reluctantly or in response to pressure – for God loves the person who gives cheerfully, and God will generously provide all you need.

God wants you to be out of debt. Proverbs 22:7 (TEV) states, "Poor people are slaves of the rich. Borrow money and you are the lender's slave." In Nehemiah 5:3-5 (NASB), the people indicated "we are making mortgages," and by doing so, "we are forcing our sons and our daughters to be slaves."

The best way to be out of debt is by not going into debt. Some of you, however, are already in debt because of college grants, etc., which you have to repay. We trust that this Kwick Kourse on Kash Kontrol will help you develop a plan to get out of debt and stay out of debt.

For now, realize these three things: God wants you to have plenty, God wants you to be able to give to others, and God wants you to be out of debt. If you believe these premises, you will be jumping into the Kwickstart lane.

Three Things God Wants You to Do

God wants you to depend on Him. Matthew 7:24-27 teaches us that trusting in anything other than God is like putting our dependency upon shifting sand. Only Jesus, the Rock, can be depended on. Also, Matthew 6:33 tells us that if we put our priority on godly things, then all "these other things" will be given to us.

Do not ever think that whoever pays your salary is your source. Do not ever think that the Church is your provider. Do not come to a false conclusion that *things* are your security. God wants each of us to come to the realization and the actualization that *He alone* is our freedom, including our financial freedom. There are things in life Mom or Dad cannot take care of for you, government cannot do, insurance cannot pay, and money cannot buy. But there is *nothing* that is beyond the reach of God's provision. He wants you willfully to place your dependency on Him.

God wants you to learn self-control. In every area of your life, God wants you to learn self-control, to discipline yourself. Paul, in 1 Corinthians 9:27, says he brings himself under control. Discipline is a principle God wants you to learn, and He uses self-control in your finances as a way of teaching you.

One thing you will have to learn is to distinguish between needs, wants, and desires. Your *needs* are your basic requirements, such as food, clothing, housing, and medical coverage. 1 Timothy 6:8 (NLT) says, "So if we have enough food and clothing, let us be content."

Your *wants* have to do with quality. For example, hamburger is food and could be listed under a need, but steak would be considered a *want*. Or an older, used but serviceable car would be considered a need in the transportation area, but a shiny new Oldsmobile convertible would be a want. 1 Peter 3:3 (NLT) says, "Don't be concerned about the outward beauty that depends on fancy hairstyles, expensive jewelry, or beautiful clothes."

Desires – according to Larry Burkett in *The Financial Planning Workbook* (Moody Press, Chicago, 1982) – are choices according to God's plan that can be made only out of surplus funds after all other obligations have been met. God wants you to learn self-control in the handling of your finances, and differentiating among needs, wants, and desires is a good way to begin.

God wants you to be charitable. God wants you to have a heart (a desire) for the poor, the fatherless, and the widows. He wants you to have an attitude of caring, of giving. Galatians 2:10 tells us that we should remember the poor.

1 Timothy 5:8 tells us that anyone who does not take care of his own family first is worse than an infidel. When financial situations do not allow you to give, having a giving attitude in your heart will help you to be creative in finding ways to give of your time, your energy, your emotional support, etc., to help meet the needs of those around you.

To be able to give financial assistance, you must learn to stay out of debt and to manage your money. We will talk about that in the next section of this chapter, where we give practical advice for the minister's wife. But for now, please understand that God wants the seed of the desire to be charitable to grow in your spirit.

Three Words of Practical Advice

Plan today for your tomorrow. Until they have developed lifetime goals, most people will not have a deep enough commitment for the day-to-day practice of financial management they must develop. You and your spouse should take a few weeks to pray and ask God what His goals are for your lives; then take some time from the everyday affairs of life and seriously establish some goals for your lives. When you have these goals set, then both of you can conscientiously work toward achieving them.

Some of these goals might be to provide college education for your children, to be out of debt, to have a comfortable retirement income, to be able to leave an inheritance for your children, or all of the above.

Please do not wait a day longer to make some provisions for the future. If you are a young person, waiting until you "make more money" will not do it. You must learn to manage the money you make *now,* so that you will have money to manage later. If you are middle-aged, it is never too late to begin. Start now.

Stay out of the parsonage. This doesn't mean "don't pastor a church," but it does mean that if there is any way on earth a church will pay you a housing allowance (talk to a tax person about special provisions the IRS makes for housing allowances) or allow you to rent the parsonage they supply, then do it. A host of retired ministers today do not have homes of their own because they lived in parsonages all their lives and felt as if they were getting a good deal. By purchasing your own home, even with a mortgage, you are building equity, and this equity grows every year. Equity is something you own. If you are living in a home provided by someone else, you own nothing! So take this word of practical advice, and stay out of the parsonage.

Practice Money Management. Aha, at last we come to the crux of the matter. Practicing money management means "setting a budget and sticking with it, no matter what." Only if you believe God wants you to succeed, believe He will give you wisdom (James 1:5), and believe that He will give you miracles to accomplish what He wants in your life, can you make yourself a budget and stick with it.

You will not be able to create a workable budget until you know exactly where your money is going now. So for the next month, both you and your spouse should write down every single penny you spend, and total it into categories.

Then you should total every source of regular income for the month. Take that total and divide it by 10. That will give a figure for 10 percent of your income and will be the amount you pay each month as your tithe. Remember, you are not actually giving anything by paying your tithe – you are just giving back to God what is rightfully His. But by giving Him what is His, you can claim the promise in Proverbs 3:9-10, which tells us that if we honor God with our "firstfruits," i.e., give our tithe off the top, then He will honor us by giving us of His plenty. Personally, I like God's plenty!

Next, list every other obligation you have. That will include taxes, housing, utilities, food, automobile payments, insurance payments, and debt payments.

To help you make sure money is on hand to pay insurance, savings for another car, or other payments that may come only once or twice a year, you can try a little trick my husband and I used: subtract that amount out of your checkbook every month, and keep a total of those subtractions in the back of your checkbook. You are not so likely to spend the money if you can't see it in your balance. You will just have to take that total into consideration, however, when you reconcile your bank statement at the end of every month. And please *do* reconcile that bank statement monthly.

Your final step will be to determine how much money, if any, is left over after the needs are paid for. This will be money you can spend on offerings to God, savings, entertainment, recreation, clothing, etc.

By doing this, you will probably see where debt has gotten you ensnared. Hopefully, this will encourage you to cut up your credit cards and begin buying things *only* when you have saved enough money to pay for them. Credit card financing eats up your income. Elect to have only one credit card. The value of having one credit card is to consolidate your payments each month so you can pay them in one check at the end of the month, i.e., pay off the total of the card at the end of each month. This way there will be no finance charges.

Here's what finance charges look like on a credit card. If you have a card debt of $5000 at the rate of 18 percent per year, you will have to pay $75 each month just to cover the interest. That is $75 per month *before* you even begin to reduce your indebtedness.

The only indebtedness you should allow yourself to have would be on your home or your car. Even then, you should buy a house or car you can truly afford, remembering there will be upkeep on both, and getting the shortest term possible can save you a lot of interest. After paying off the car you have now, plan to pay cash for your next one.

Invest in a Larry Burkett book on financial planning (there are several), or buy the book *The Debt-FREE & Prosperous Living Basic Course* by John Commuta (Marketline Press, Wauzeka, Wisconsin, 1997) to help prepare a budget you can live with that will set you on your way to being debt free. Financial freedom is in God's plan for you, and He will help you achieve it.

Three Results of Living God's Way

Rightness. Romans 14:17 tells us that the kingdom of God is not meat nor drink, but righteousness, peace, and joy. Another meaning of that Greek word for righteousness is "rightness." Remember, the Word says that if we seek first the things of God, then all these other things will be added unto us. Reaching for your goals, being free from the slavery of debt, and enjoying the "other things" will bring a sense of rightness to your world.

Rest. A rest that is a gift to the children of God (Hebrews 4:9) comes from having your finances in order, from giving God what belongs to Him, and from being able to give unselfishly to those in need. It is a peace that passes all understanding.

Rejoicing. A rejoicing comes when you know you have been the faithful and wise steward Luke referred to when he said "whom the Lord will make ruler over all that he has." Joy is an inevitable by-product of Korrectly Kontrolling the Kash over which God has made you the ruler.

Take heart, sister in Christ. Pay your bills and keep out of debt – good advice for all!

Necessary

Importance of Prayer and Bible Study
for the Minister's Wife

by Dayna Belcher

People can tell when someone is in love. "She just *glows*" is the description we hear. What is being in love, anyway? Some say being in love is finding that *special someone*, the one who seems to *fit* you like a glove, the one who was seemingly made just for you, by God, out of *all* people in the earth, the one whose eyes *lock* with yours in a crowded room, the one who makes your heart *flutter* and *race* all at the same time, the one who makes you forget what you were even thinking about before he walked into the room. That kind of love happened for me 28 years ago when I met my husband, Curtis. That kind of love is still happening between us today. Next to Jesus, he is the love of my life. Even now, time seems to pause so that I can savor moments when I get a glimpse of him. I get excited to see him and be with him anytime. I can't resist his invitations to spend time with him, whether over lunch or just being quiet in the same room together. He is a costly, priceless, one-of-a-kind, irreplaceable treasure to me.

> *When Moses came down from Mount Sinai with the two tablets of the Testimony in his hands, he was not aware that his face was radiant because he had spoken with the Lord. When Aaron and all the Israelites saw Moses, his face was radiant, and they were afraid to come near him. But Moses called to them; so Aaron and all the leaders of the community came back to him, and*

he spoke to them. Afterward all the Israelites came near him, and he gave them all the commands the Lord had given him on Mount Sinai (Exodus 34:29-32, NIV).

Scripture records that Moses glowed when he descended from Mt. Sinai following his time spent in communion, prayer, counsel, and instruction with the Lord God.

Prayer takes on many forms. It can come about through thought, words, groaning when we cannot find the words, tears, rejoicing and laughter before the Lord, as well as speaking His Word back to Him in communication. Following are just a few of these forms and expressions.

Prayer is the very breath that our relationship with Him travels upon. It connects heaven and earth – our spirit to His Spirit! It is the vehicle transcending *all* possible gaps and chasms in our relationship to Holy God. Prayer is our key to intimacy with the Father, through the passageway of Jesus Christ, His Son. To me, to breathe is to pray, and to pray is to breathe. To think upon Him, to ponder His wonder and greatness, is not only necessary, but also life-giving and life-receiving. All glory and all honor due His name are expressed, and our incapacity for perfection is divinely overshadowed by *His* perfection, so that all He sees is Himself, covering us with all that He is, hiding in the Shadow of His Presence all that we are not. The fullness of our time spent together is rich and satisfying not only to us, but to *God* Himself. Just as He spoke with Adam and Eve, just as He spoke with Moses and Abraham, He is here waiting to speak to us through the gift of communication in prayer and His Word.

Prayer is a precious gift from God to us. Jesus demonstrated for His disciples how to communicate with the Father in heaven through prayer. He taught them to pray. Not only is prayer a gift *from* God to us through Jesus Christ, His Son, but it is also our gift *to* God. To pray is to acknowledge Him as Supreme. Through prayer, we acknowledge His supremacy and our total dependency upon Him as His creation.

How many of us leap inside for joy when we are sought out, called by name, and removed from the place of blending in and going unnoticed to a place of being recognized and brought to the forefront? To feel such warmth of love, acceptance, and a sense of "I'm someone *special* – they *know* me and recognize me as a *person*; they call me by name" is incredible! It is love and respect in action. It is such kindness, such hospitality extended.

Two of our greatest needs as human beings are to be loved by others and to love others. It is powerful to understand that the Lord God Himself longs for us to recognize *Him* and call *Him* by name. I believe that He feels this way when we pray to Him. He has a need to love us and to be loved by us, His creation. We have a need to love Him and for Him to love us. The Word instructs us to not pray in vain repetitions. We must be determined to seek Him in spirit and in truth, coming before Him simply as we are and giving ourselves freely to Him.

> ***Prayer Point:*** *Ponder prayer as a gift from God. Ponder prayer offered up as a gift from us to Him. Ponder prayer as a gift to God from us on a daily, moment-by-moment basis; as a place of living, a place of understanding, and a dwelling place in our minds as we go about our daily of dailies.*

Prayer is a daily giving of ourselves to God in communion and communication. Yet so often, we think of it as seeking Him simply for answers to our requests. When we pray, we are positioning ourselves in humility and total dependence before the living God, incapable in ourselves of accomplishing anything in this life without Him. I believe He absolutely loves it when we communicate with Him and submit to who He is in all His wonder! He longs for that from humankind. *"I am the vine; you are the branches. If a man remains in me and I in him, he will bear much fruit; apart from me you can do nothing"* (John 15:5, NIV).

59

There was no way for Moses to be with God as he was and not have a literal glow as a manifestation and testament of the time they had shared together. The fact that the glow did not last, but faded, tells us that we need to go before the Lord time and time again, keeping the fires of love and devotion ever burning to our God. Moses' living temple *encased* a memento, a souvenir, a temporary keepsake, if you will, of having been in the best place of all – in the presence of Almighty God! When we touch heaven, we come away glowing with the glory of heaven's light. We light up as a result of Jesus' very presence having met with us right where we are. We are changed as we experience this "glory to glory" that 2 Corinthians 3:18-19 speaks about.

> *And all of us, with unveiled faces, seeing the glory*
> *of the Lord as though reflected in a mirror, are being*
> *transformed into the same image from one degree of*
> *glory to another; for this comes from the Lord, the Spirit*
> (2 Corinthians 3:18, NRSV).

> *I did not see a temple in the city, because the Lord God*
> *Almighty and the Lamb are its temple. The city does not*
> *need the sun or the moon to shine on it, for the glory of God*
> *gives it light, and the Lamb is its lamp. The nations will*
> *walk by its light, and the kings of the earth will bring their*
> *splendor into it* (Revelation 21:22-24, NIV).

When we are passionately in love, we cannot hide it. It glimmers from within us for all to see. Intentionally seeking out Jesus to spend time with Him, talking, listening, singing, receiving instruction, laughing, crying, and being silent before Him – what an explosive thought!

> **Prayer Point:** *What would happen if we intentionally*
> *pursued the One who is love, Jesus Christ, rather than*
> *expecting our prayer life and time in the Word to come about*
> *by happenstance? Ask yourself what changes would occur.*

We must understand that Jesus is crazy about us, interested in giving us the best of Himself, and longing to be in constant communion with us. When we understand that, we know that passion and wisdom have been both awakened in and multiplied to us. I believe that just as our heart leaps with joy when our love walks through the door, so does the heart of the Bridegroom leap when He sees us coming to Him. I believe He says, "*That's* My girl! *There* she is!" In those moments, when we encounter Him and spend time alone with Him, it is as if His love is being squeezed out onto us as a heavy, expensive perfume being expressed from a heavenly sponge. He saturates us with love; His love is *lavished* upon us. When we think of those times, we remember the fragrance. We are able to find each other by that *same* fragrance each time we meet.

Though Scripture tells us in Psalm 139 that God is everywhere – omnipresent – still, I believe He loves it when we cry out in desperation after Him, "Jesus, how can I *find* You today? I *need* You. I *long* to be with You ... to *speak* with You ... to *love* You today. Come *be* with me! Share Your heart with me. This is what is going on with me. Teach me. Reveal my heart. Lay it bare before You, that I may ask You to make it more like Yours. Show me Your mysteries that I know not of, as Your Word says."

"O God, you are my God, earnestly I seek you; my soul thirsts for you, my body longs for you, in a dry and weary land where there is no water" (Psalm 63:1, NIV).

Jesus is the Redeemer, Life-giver, and Lover to whom we are betrothed. Jesus is Love, and He extended that love long ago as the ultimate sacrifice. Today, He is still extending that love to each one of us. Many steeped in religion still miss His call today. He beckons to us – His love song to Himself – humankind. Awaken to the understanding that you are His best writing, His most exquisite love song, His one-and-only, irreplaceable piece of art He has created for Himself. He completely loves who you are – your personality that He formed uniquely in you. He loves your style and expression. It is unique, different from any other in the earth. Release yourself to Him! Call upon Him, and He will meet you where you are in life-giving and truly matchless communion.

Religion has killed many things that once teemed with life. Religious people busy themselves with lifeless stencils and forms, dreaming of days long ago, rather than anticipating and expecting the all-powerful One, Jesus Christ, and His move *for* now, *in* the now – *the Bridegroom coming!* Religion without relationship tempts us to live in the past rather than to be looking for the Groom, Jesus Christ.

It is time to go from merely existing, striving, and barely surviving to thriving in His presence and Himself revealed. In this beautiful exchange, Jesus gives the breath of His Spirit to our lifeless forms. It is time now to arise and live! Be awakened as the bride to her Groom! Receive the fresh breath of His Spirit!

> *The hand of the Lord was upon me, and he brought me out by the Spirit of the Lord and set me in the middle of a valley; it was full of bones. He led me back and forth among them, and I saw a great many bones on the floor of the valley, bones that were very dry. He asked me, "Son of man, can these bones live?"*
>
> *I said, "O Sovereign Lord, you alone know."*
>
> *Then he said to me, "Prophesy to these bones and say to them, 'Dry bones, hear the word of the Lord! This is what the Sovereign Lord says to these bones: I will make breath enter you, and you will come to life. I will attach tendons to you and make flesh come upon you and cover you with skin; I will put breath in you, and you will come to life. Then you will know that I am the Lord.'"*
>
> *So I prophesied as I was commanded. And as I was prophesying, there was a noise, a rattling sound, and the bones came together, bone to bone. I looked, and tendons and flesh appeared on them and skin covered them, but there was no breath in them.*

Then he said to me, "Prophesy to the breath; prophesy,
son of man, and say to it, 'This is what the Sovereign
Lord says: Come from the four winds, O breath, and
breathe into these slain, that they may live.'" So I
prophesied as he commanded me, and breath entered
them; they came to life and stood up on their feet – a
vast army (Ezek 37:1-10, NIV).

Can you *hear* it? Can you *hear* the beginnings of the heavenly bridal chorus playing, or do you simply hear, "To-do-do-do-do ... To-do-dos"? The Lover of Your Soul awaits retrieval of His bride, the church, and her arrival into His arms of love and their heavenly home together for eternity. The wedding rehearsal is *now*. I exhort you to fall in love with the One who desperately loves you. Fall in love again and again and again. Marvel at Him! Adore Him! Find that place on the altar of abandonment and surrender! From that place will come strategy and overcoming strength for this life. Can you hear the Bridegroom now gently beckoning to His bride, "Come. Awaken, My morning dove! I've appointed commissioners to awaken you to My love. Hear Me calling you. Come! Come!"

But Martha was cumbered about much serving, and
came to him, and said, Lord, dost thou not care that
my sister hath left me to serve alone? bid her therefore
that she help me. And Jesus answered and said unto her,
Martha, Martha, thou art careful and troubled about
many things: But one thing is needful: and Mary hath
chosen that good part, which shall not be taken away
from her (Luke 10:40-42).

I encourage you to trade your "To-dos" and your weary working for endless "Mary" days and nights of passionate conversation and Word revelation between the engaged couple, that is, the coming Bridegroom and His bride. When Martha complained to Jesus about Mary's not helping her, as recorded in Luke 10, Jesus said of Mary in His reply, "She has chosen the best part."

Drink of the endless cup of His presence. Prepare your garments for His Presence, and receive the gifts your betrothed lavishes upon you in this hour. Accept His love. None of us is worthy. Let His worthiness cover all of your unworthiness, and enter in freely! That is prayer. That is encounter. That is the place to dwell.

"It is finished! I am the A and the Z – the Beginning and the End. I will give to the thirsty the springs of the Water of Life – as a gift!" (Revelation 21:6, TLB) Over the years, I have prayed, asking God not to let me die among the dead, but let me die among the living! I have found Him, the Way, the Truth, the Life – that is, Jesus. I live and thrive in Him, and I will die without His presence. That is passion. That is vital to my survival as a Christian and as a minister. Do not turn me away from my Lover, the Maker of the Heavens and the Earth! I long for Him, and He longs for time with me. I long for His return. I must pour out my soul to the One who poured out His life for me. I give my life daily to Him, as He gave His first for me. He chose me. He chose you. We stand in agreement, my spirit with His Spirit. That is relationship. That is vital. You must have understanding of this wonderful relationship to live.

Oh, the countless wonderings and ponderings in His presence, marveling at Him and the world He created. Hearing how much He loves me and why He made me just as I am causes my heart to pound and my spirit to leap with joy at such revelation. I hear Him sing over me with joy and woo me to go past insecurity and elevation of "I can't," doubts, those things that say that they are impassable and impossible.

Let us go from being lovers of self and exalting insecurities to emerge as a confident bride who has found herself totally covered in His perfection. Let us break every engagement to lifeless forms and purposes to remain true to our betrothed, Jesus – engaged to *Life!* Let us accept His love. Let us accept His call. Let us walk with Him, and Him with us.

Prayer Point: *Is this necessary? Yes. Is this vital? Yes. Will I do it? Yes! Am I now? Yes, yes, yes! Will you? Are you now?*

Then when you call upon me and come and pray to me, I will hear you. When you search for me, you will find me; if you seek me with all your heart, I will let you find me, says the Lord, and I will restore your fortunes and gather you from all the nations and all the places where I have driven you, says the Lord, and I will bring you back to the place from which I sent you into exile (Jeremiah 29:12-14, NRSV).

Jesus is inviting you and me in this hour, "Come away with Me." As we get lost in Him, losing sight of ourselves, going past our pain and concerns, higher than drain and burnout, we can drink the cup of His presence into our sun-scorched souls. It is in that state of communion, where He pours the oil of His presence from the high place of heaven and the deep place of His heart into our very beings, that He causes us to live again and thrive. Being with Him in prayer, in the revelation of His Word, causes us to see only Him and to hear His directives and the love songs He sings over us in our hearts. To be with Him, to encounter Him, is to stir up love more and more, causing us to melt before Him in passion of communion! We find ourselves in abandonment and the spiritual intoxication of His Presence in the worship of Him who was and is and is to come. We are to live out the promise of forever in the now. That is relationship. That is necessary.

"I am the Alpha and the Omega," says the Lord God, "who is, and who was, and who is to come, the Almighty" (Revelation 1:8, NIV).

STRUGGLES

- ***Not My Boy!***

- ***When the Unthinkable Happens***

- ***The "W" Word***

Not My Boy!

Substance Abuse in the Pastor's Home

by Judith Phelps

It was a beautiful fall day, Thursday, October 5, 1995, and I was home alone. I'd cleaned and made preparation for my husband Maurice's return home the following evening from a hunting trip with our older son, Daryle.

October 5 has been an easy date for me to remember since 1974. That was my due date for my younger son, Keith, and, like all mothers, I always remembered the due date of my children as easily as their birth date. It's just one of those "mom things." Keith arrived five days late, October 10, 1974, and we were delighted to be blessed with another son.

Although Keith was an exceptionally good baby, it didn't take us long to learn that he was one with a mind of his own. There was something fascinating to him about trying the things he had been warned against. However, other than school mischief, a couple of speeding violations, and a small traffic accident at 16, he made it through school without getting into trouble.

Keith had always been drawn to amusement parks with a strong desire to work at one. So it was, after graduating from high school in 1992, that he left the family nest in Morehead City, North Carolina, to pursue his dream at King's Dominion just outside Richmond, Virginia. The promise was that after a year out of school, he would enroll in college. Needless to say, he loved the much faster pace Richmond and the surrounding area had to offer versus the slower pace of life in our beach and fishing village. In 1993, when the amusement park pay wasn't sufficient to make ends meet, he accepted a job with a bank. College was still on hold.

Another fascination in Keith's life has always been music, so when a friend who mixed music and worked as a DJ for a nightclub offered to help him learn that particular skill, he took her up on it. He's a lover of sound technology and electronics and learned quickly. In fact, he was so good at it that in the spring of 1995 he moved to Washington, D.C., where he accepted a job as DJ in a nightclub.

Moms and dads (particularly moms) have this special sense of radar. We're like a hound dog when it comes to smelling trouble, and trouble was coming. Maurice and I warned and prayed about all the enticing and dangerous things available, especially in the larger cities, but each time anything was mentioned, the sort of answer we got from Keith was, "It's a job. I do my thing, and they do theirs."

Maurice had just met with Keith for a visit at Maurice's parents' home one month earlier and noticed he seemed a little thinner than usual. Then, that dreadful night of October 5, just as I was preparing to go to bed, the phone rang. What I heard – "This is Joe Marcus (name changed). I thought you needed to know that Keith is addicted to heroin and possibly another drug even though he has asked me not to say anything to you. He said he'd tell you after he weans himself off" – gave me such a sinking, gut-wrenching feeling. Disbelief *(Not MY boy!)*, fear, and panic gripped me. My mind raced forward to questions of the future and what we were to face, and backward with *What did we do wrong? How have we failed as parents?* All of this was later followed with feelings of anger, grief, and more questions, but first things first; I had to greet Maurice at the airport with a smile and a kiss before getting him in a private place and dropping the bomb on him.

We met, we kissed, we got in a private place and talked. We cried and planned. What could we possibly do? How could we "fix it"? Mothers particularly have this need to fix it for their children – put a Band-Aid on it, kiss it, make the pain go away. Do something! Do *anything!*

Prayer Point: God, help me to realize every day that, although we are given the task of raising our children in the knowledge and understanding of You, the actions of our adult children are their responsibility. Remove the burden of guilt.

Our first plan of action was to phone Keith and tell him we'd be coming up to Washington to celebrate his 21st birthday the following week. I kept my word of not telling him I knew of his plight. Arrangements were made, and Maurice and I were off to Washington to celebrate Keith's birthday as best we could, to confront, and to encourage him to take action by seeking help for his addiction.

When we arrived, we found a very thin, hollow-faced, hollow-eyed son. He stands 6'1", and his pants (size 29-30" waist) were somewhat loose. Joe had confessed his phone call, so Keith was prepared for his defense of wanting to try to conquer this addiction on his own before giving up everything and going for treatment. As far as we saw it, he had already given up everything for drugs, but we could do nothing but return home heavy-hearted and rev up those prayers for him.

For a number of weeks, we didn't tell our immediate families or our church family, other than a select few who we knew would hold the info totally confidential and not act as judges, but pray for Keith and us. Truthfully, it was hard to know how to tell others. Somehow I just couldn't muster the strength or courage to say, "Keith is a heroin addict." There was a lot of processing Maurice and I needed to do. So we kept quiet and tried to put on a good front, although inside we were screaming for help.

Prayer Point: God, give me the grace to ask for help when I need it. Release me from the fear of man, and teach me to be transparent with those who would come alongside and lift me up in arms of love.

71

Within a few days of our return home from the birthday/confrontation visit, Keith phoned to ask if I would be willing to come stay with him for a few days and help him go "cold turkey." Of course I would! I agreed to pack some things and leave the following morning. Fortunately, I work in the church office, so getting away from the job for a few days wasn't difficult for me to work out. I contacted a local physician's assistant friend and asked for any info he could give me on helping someone go off heroin cold turkey and what to expect. He dropped off some information and warned me to be careful – for example, the blood pressure could go dangerously high, and he cautioned that Keith could possibly become violent. Knowing all of that didn't deter me at all. I had a mission to accomplish – help my son free himself of drug addiction. (Oh, how little we knew at the time! As the old saying goes, "It's easier said than done.") I also armed myself with my Bible, a counselor's handbook, and anything that I thought might help me through this time. I knew absolutely no one in Washington to call on for counsel, encouragement, or prayer. It was going to be me, Keith, and God.

When I arrived Keith, looked even worse than he had a week earlier. I got settled in, and we got right down to business. It didn't take long for withdrawal symptoms, the worst of which last approximately 36 hours, to set in. Withdrawal symptoms include dilated pupils, goose bumps, watery eyes, runny nose, yawning, loss of appetite, vomiting, tremors, panic, chills, sweating, nausea, severe muscle cramps, and insomnia. As withdrawal progresses, elevations in blood pressure, pulse, respiratory rate, and temperature occur.

For approximately 16 hours, I watched Keith experience probably all of the above symptoms. I stayed by his side all night long, promising not to leave him (he was afraid), and massaging his feet, legs, arms, etc. so as to help him get as much rest as possible. The muscle cramps were the most noticeable. I'm not talking about a minor leg cramp. I'm talking about muscles throughout the entire body. The spasms were constant, and they became so severe that he said he couldn't take it any longer. He insisted on going out to buy more drugs, and even though I protested, having some sound mind left, I didn't try to stop him forcefully. I just sat there and cried and prayed for God to take care of him and help us find another way.

When Keith returned to his apartment, he was already feeling better physically but still wanted help, so we started making plans to find a hospital that would accept him for detox, thinking they would surely give him something to relieve the awful withdrawal symptoms. For a week, we went round and round with his insurance company, doing everything they told us to do in order for him to be admitted to a hospital in Annapolis, Maryland. By the end of the week, Keith was running out of money, as he had reached the point he was not able to work. Knowing I wouldn't be buying any drugs, we phoned the hospital and asked if they would admit him the following day. They agreed.

The next morning, a Friday, Keith took his last shot of heroin, and I drove him to Annapolis. We arrived around lunch, and the admitting process was a story within itself. I finally told the admitting clerk to forget the insurance company, and I wrote a check to cover his four-day stay.

Once that was taken care of, I went a few blocks away and checked myself into a motel. By then, I felt mentally, physically, emotionally, and spiritually exhausted. I felt all alone. My few days with Keith at that point had turned into 2½ weeks. Little did I know that our struggle was just beginning. Had I been able to see what was ahead, I don't think I could have made it. Thank goodness, God gives us strength for today and hope for tomorrow.

Because of some health problems, Maurice had stayed at home doing all he could to keep things going and "looking normal" while I "was spending a little time with Keith helping him deal with a problem." I phoned and asked him to join me for the weekend because I felt that I couldn't go it alone any longer. Then I got on my knees by my bed and cried out to

God. I told him how desperate I was, how cold I was (it was beginning to snow outside), and how alone I felt with my son in a detox hospital going through hell, and me several hundred miles from home and family. In fact, I had never felt so alone in my life. Suddenly, I sensed the Lord's presence. It was as if warm arms engulfed me and a peace settled over me. I knew I could make it.

I got up and went back to the hospital to attend a support group that evening provided for family members. Much love and support were shown to me by several individuals there when they learned I was so far from home and family. I recall the leader asking each of us what we had done within the past week *just for ourselves*. All I could think of was the fact that I had brought along several *Readers' Digest* magazines, and I had taken a few minutes here and there to read nothing but the funny stories/quotes. I love humor, and I think it was at that moment I realized ... if there was any humor to be found, I'd better find it because I was going to need all I could get. From then on, no matter how difficult things got at times, I looked for any humor in the situation.

Maurice arrived on Saturday, and we spent the weekend in and out of the hospital with Keith. It was difficult watching him suffer withdrawal again, but it seemed to help him somewhat just having us there. He had thought the hospital would give him medication to help with the symptoms, but not so. However, they did monitor him carefully.

Keith was released on Monday afternoon. The three of us traveled back to Washington to pick up some of his things and then go on to our home in Morehead City. We spent a l-o-n-g night in a motel, with Maurice getting up in the middle of the night to take Keith out to eat. He was constantly needing to use the restroom and wanting something to eat (a withdrawal symptom we didn't know about). Although he had come through the worst 36 hours of withdrawal, none of us realized it would take many days longer for the drugs to get completely out of his system.

Due to the lingering effects of the drugs making it impossible to deal with Keith at home (his father sat with him all night on his first night home), we had him admitted to a 30-day drug rehabilitation facility within three days. His first week was a struggle, but the remaining three weeks went relatively well. On graduation day, Keith thought he had it all under control now, so he left to return to Washington. He crashed immediately!

By now, it was December, and Christmas was a nightmare. We realized that we needed all the love, prayers, and support our immediate family and church family could possibly give us. The Lord sent encouragement along the way from family and friends, as well as through His Word and articles we read. An example of that came when I attended a T. D. Jakes seminar in March of '96. I went *expecting* to hear from God. When the doors opened, I hurriedly found my way to a seat near the front. I certainly didn't want to be in the back if God had something for me! As Pastor Jakes spoke that night, he suddenly stopped and said, *"I don't know who this is for, but God said, 'This is your year. Your son is coming home.'"* I didn't do any cartwheels, and I didn't know who else needed that word, but I accepted it for me and held on to it.

One month later, Keith phoned and asked if he could come home to "get his life together." He arrived home on a Sunday morning, with the help of three precious individuals from our church who drove all night to get him. He was not drug free, but he was home and attended church with us for the first time in three years.

The struggle was hard, very hard. Keith wanted to be free, but he wanted/needed drugs. He recommitted his life to Christ and attended church faithfully, but he still craved. That summer, he started making up and writing his own prescriptions. He knew plenty about which medications would stop his cravings, because he had been on pain killers during a 2½-week hospital stay in 1993 for a collapsed lung and then again in 1994; and on the Internet and in books, he had studied the effects of drugs.

It wasn't long before Keith was caught. He received probation and was soon caught again. He went for more short-term rehabilitation, came home, and was caught again. In 1997, I spent practically the entire year shuffling my schedule so I could go to court with him. All of this while trying to work part-time, keep house, and help plan for our older son's wedding. Keith was caught for passing forged prescriptions in four North Carolina counties as well as one in Virginia. Maurice and I did not pay for any lawyers and did not bail him out of jail, but I wouldn't give up on him and allow him to go to court alone. I spent hours on the road with Keith and in courtrooms that year.

During the time not spent on the road, there were some positives in Keith's life. He worked in our maintenance department at the church. He became friends with a young deaf man while in one of the several rehab centers he attended. This young man helped him start learning sign language, so Keith enrolled in a communications class at our local community college. He assisted in signing to the deaf in our worship services here at Glad Tidings Church. He also attended support groups and counseling and made some wonderful, supportive Christian friends.

However, by December 1997, things were no better as far as cravings and forging prescriptions were concerned, so Keith went to Teen Challenge. When Maurice and I visited him after one month, we were pleased with what we saw happening in his life – he looked like a new man, had a different attitude, and talked about his devotional life and relationship with God – but after 2½ more months, Keith phoned to say he was leaving. Hindsight says we shouldn't have allowed him to do that and come back home, but we did.

He got a job at Radio Shack and loved it, but it wasn't long before Keith was back to his same old habits. Although he was trying hard to do all the right things, Satan was still on his heels. In February 1999, Keith wrote a prescription for someone who said, "You owe me the favor." He was caught and sent to prison for 2½ years.

During this time, we had dear and supportive friends who asked about Keith regularly and kept us encouraged. Some wrote and visited him, and there were a few who asked him to phone them occasionally (all calls had to be collect). Only God will ever know how truly grateful Maurice and I are for the many kindnesses shown to us and Keith during this time.

September 11, 2001 – Who could forget that day?! It's forever engraved in the minds of every American. For us it was a bittersweet day. It was Keith's release date from prison. Maurice and I arrived at 8:40 a.m. We waited at a little shelter, something like a school bus stop, for him to come out. As the wait became quite long, a guard stopped by to ask if we had heard the awful news of a plane crash in New York. In a few minutes, the same guard stopped again to tell us of a second crash. By then, we were wondering if Keith was going to get out of there. At 10:00 a.m., Keith walked free! A few days later, we learned that almost immediately following his release, the prison ordered "shutdown," which meant that had he not gotten out when he did, he would not have been able to leave for some time, as this shutdown was due to all the horrible tragedies of 9/11.

I wish I could say that when Keith walked free from that prison, he also walked free from the prison of drug abuse and that we all lived happily ever after. But in the summer of 2002, he moved to Greenville, North Carolina, to live in a halfway house and work. The halfway house situation was not good, and work was scarce for him. Loneliness, stress, lack of money, among other things, are not good for anyone, much less an addict, to face, so Keith went back to writing prescriptions for medication that would help him "not care."

During this time, he was kicked out of another halfway house for drug use and had no place to go but a homeless shelter. How painful for Maurice and me to know that we live in a nice home, own two vehicles and a camper, and have nice clothes and plenty to eat, but our precious son was still in the pigpen, and we knew we had to let him stay there!

Keith was again caught passing a prescription, and this time he asked if he could be allowed to go to a long-term treatment facility. Had the normal process of law transpired, Keith would have been sentenced to prison again for a longer period of time. However, God was merciful. The judge, district attorney, probation officer, and Keith's attorney all agreed on sending him for the long-term treatment. He went and stayed for 14 months.

Upon leaving this facility, Keith moved to Raleigh, where today he is working full-time and continuing his education. He's an A student and is earning his degree in information technology. He is enrolled in a methadone clinic near where he lives. I know there are a lot of people who question using methadone —"It's trading one chemical dependency for another." That is true. But the damage was done to Keith's system years back, when he first made the wrong choice to try drugs and became addicted to heroin. Methadone does *not* give Keith a "high." In fact, if he took heroin or some other opiate drug, the methadone would block its effect. He takes one daily dose and is able to function without craving and is happy to have some normalcy to his life. Also, he is now free of supervised probation for the first time since 1996.

There were many other events too numerous and some too heartbreaking for a mother to share here, but one should understand that substance abuse in any home is a difficult road to walk.

Although at times Keith and Daryle's relationship was strained due to letdown ("He was raised to know better"), anger ("He's humiliating the whole family"), and heartache ("He's killing himself and Mom and Dad with him"), Daryle continued to love unconditionally, and they have a good relationship today.

One may wonder about our pride ... the embarrassment and humiliation of all this. Well, we kicked all that out the door a long time ago. Our son's health and his soul are more important than what people think about us.

Maurice and I continue to believe for complete healing in Keith's life. He is a very smart, loving, and caring guy with a great sense of humor. Keith does profess to be a Christian, and, apart from his drug problem, he was never involved with the law in any situations other than the traffic offenses mentioned earlier. We were blessed that he never stole from us or anyone else to provide for his addiction.

We give God praise and glory for sustaining us all through this long, dark night in our lives. Today, we may not be as strong physically, but we are stronger in our relationship with Christ, and He has helped us be able to minister to others in a way we never could have before.

> ***Prayer Point:*** *Lord, remind me to give glory and praise to you, not only for visible miracles, but also for strength, sustenance, and your presence with us during the dark night of trials.*

We do not know what the future holds, but we definitely know Who holds the future, and by the eye of faith, Maurice and I believe our son Keith will become free in any area of his life that holds him in bondage, that he will prosper, and that he will be a great witness for Christ and the up-building of His Kingdom. Until then, I stand on this Word: *"I have seen his ways, and will heal him: I will lead him also, and restore comforts unto him and to his mourners"* (Isaiah 57:18).

When the Unthinkable Happens

A Story of Hope, Renewal, Restoration, and Victory

by Margaret Stone

I remember how cold it was that February morning, but the outside temperature was mild compared to the icy fingers of shock, anger, and horror that gripped my heart. My husband, after more than 20 years of marriage, stood in our bedroom and confessed his violation of our marriage vows. My world crumbled at my feet as I stared blankly at the man I thought I knew.

Ray and I married young – I was 19, and he was 20. Both of us were strong Christians and had a common goal: to give ourselves fully to the work of the Lord. Our zeal for God and a heart for His kingdom helped us to be diligent in whatever our hands found to do. This included preaching weekend meetings, youth camps, vacation Bible schools, and street ministry with a rescue mission. The love we had for each other was only strengthened by our love for the Lord and His work. No sacrifice would be too great in order to obey His voice.

Our first official ministry position was as pastor of a small suburban church. Ray and I launched into this task full of zeal, energy, hopes, and dreams. We partnered in everything from pastoral visitation to the preaching schedule. It appeared we were ideally suited to each other and to full-time ministry. Ray's gifts and abilities were evidenced in his administrative skills and effective teaching, and I was an outgoing "people person." By all standards, for such very young people, we were successful.

Denominational leaders began to take notice of Ray. He was young and articulate, full of great potential; and over the next several years served in a variety of Christian leadership positions. During this time, our family was growing, and I enjoyed my role as a full-time mom. Our marriage exemplified a great ministry partnership.

Now, 20 years later, our responsibilities centered in a large city where, once again, we gave ourselves fully to building a successful and fruitful ministry. For years, we diligently worked night and day, directing a training center, giving pastoral oversight, leading a ministry team, and counseling, as well as home schooling our youngest daughter. We assumed our marriage was strong, and so many other things demanded attention that we hardly gave a thought to each other.

Actually, I ached for Ray's attention but felt guilty and "unspiritual" when I asked him to sacrifice "important" work to spend time with me. I thought if I prayed more, fasted more, and worked harder, God would somehow fill the aching emptiness in my heart, and I wouldn't need my husband so much. Resentment began to rear its ugly head, but I stuffed it back down, endeavoring to appear committed to the work of the Lord and willing to make any sacrifice for Him. This attitude resulted in Ray and me walking parallel but separate paths. He did his work, and I did mine. However, the painful neglect of our marriage left me emotionally weary and resentful of ministry while Ray poured more and more time and energy into the work. My heart filled with smoldering anger and bitterness.

During this period, our ministry supervisor visited our home, and I tried to work up the courage to ask for help. I gave little hints that we were stressed and overworked, often with a chuckle, but I was unable to tell him how hurt, angry, and bitter I had become. After all, my Christian leadership image was at stake. Protecting an image makes it impossible for brothers and sisters to truly know us and offer the help that is so desperately needed and that Christ has provided in the context of a community of believers. If Ray and I had opened our hearts at that time, we might have averted Satan's devastating blow.

Now, the story of the ideal ministry family ends – and a new story begins. It's a story of deep agony, shame, and humiliation. It is also a story of hope, renewal, restoration, and victory. Life as we had known it up to that cold February day was forever past, but God was at work in our distress even before we asked Him – He opened "a door of hope in the Valley of Trouble" (Hosea 2:15).

After meeting with ministry leaders, Ray and I said sad and tearful goodbyes to our friends and coworkers whom we had loved for so long and began the journey to our new life – whatever and wherever that would be. Our first destination was to see our children. They all lived and attended college in the same area, so we asked them to plan for a family meeting as soon as we arrived. Ray wanted to speak to our family face to face and not allow time for rumors uglier than the truth to reach them.

Silent questions were in their eyes as we sat in the small college apartment. Agony strained Ray's voice as he tried to find the right words to soften the dreadful news he had to share. "Kids," he began, as tears formed and fell quickly from his eyes, "I'm so sorry to tell you that I have offended God, sinned against your mother, and violated the trust that you have placed in me your entire lives. I can only throw myself on your mercy and ask for your forgiveness."

The silence seemed to last an eternity, punctuated by the catching of breath, like the sound of someone who has been punched in the stomach. Ever so painfully, Ray had chosen the right path of truth and responsibility. There was no effort to justify his action or to blame anyone else. He didn't blame stress, an inattentive wife, or pressures of the ministry. This attitude is absolutely essential if a broken life and marriage are to be completely healed. Self-justification blocks the free flow of God's grace and restoration power. After Ray's painful confession, these almost grown, incredibly mature young people stood and wrapped their arms around Ray and me together. Words wouldn't come, but tears flowed freely with the love, comfort, and forgiveness they offered.

The magnitude of that moment in the healing process cannot be described. Our children, the most important people in our lives, still loved us and would stand with us in our darkest hours. Ray and I helped the children find a friend and confidant who would help each of them deal with his own pain, anger, and disappointment. In the weeks, months, and even years that followed, they, too, grasped a new understanding of grace while they watched with faith and hope as their parents walked the long and often lonely path of restoration.

When a church leader's marriage is devastated, it touches every area of the couple's life. Of course, our job was terminated, as it should have been. Neither of us had anything left in us – spiritually or emotionally. We were empty, broken, humiliated, and ashamed. And we had no money and no place to live. Life had never appeared so bleak, and death would have been sweet relief. Somehow, I kept breathing in and out and putting one foot in front of the other. A dear friend, also a pastor's wife, constantly gave me hope and encouragement. When I thought I could never trust again, she assured me that I could and would. When I was convinced that my marriage would never be strong again, she smiled and reminded me that God was a specialist at making broken things whole.

Everywhere Ray and I went, we had to face people who knew us, loved us, and had believed in us. Because gossip travels quickly in church circles, just as it does in any other arena, there was no place to hide. Our ministry was a prominent one, so the failure was even more public. Shame and humiliation dogged our steps. A few acquaintances turned their backs and chose to avoid us, but many friends came to our rescue with love, kindness, financial help, and hopeful encouragement.

Ray made a decision right away that he would submit to whatever process of discipline our leaders chose to follow.

That choice gave me great hope because the path upward must always lead downward first. One friend advised against giving anyone that kind of power over our lives, but Ray and I knew we could not trust ourselves to handle this process. God worked through godly leadership, whose goal was restoration rather than punishment, to help us find healing for the self-inflicted wounds on our marriage and our ministries.

The Scripture offers incredible encouragement concerning discipline: "...Do not make light of the Lord's discipline, and do not lose heart when he rebukes you, because the Lord disciplines those he loves ..." (Hebrews 12:5, 6 NIV). Expressions of God's love poured in regularly from friends and family. The cards and letters and phone calls let us know that we were never alone, no matter how lonely and abandoned we might have felt.

The pain and brokenness were so severe that it was impossible for us to help ourselves, so we were thankful to have the help of a wonderful Christian counselor. The need for this kind of aid cannot be overemphasized. We needed a qualified person to help Ray dig deep to find the roots of this misconduct. And I certainly needed help to process the pain, anger, and shattered trust. A true professional, Dr. Taylor showed such kindness and wisdom during the very first visit that we left with true hope rising in our hearts. He assured us that our marriage was not beyond repair and that God had not thrown us on the rubbish heap.

Ray's road out of the ashes of despair began with deep sorrow and repentance. Many people find that path repulsive, but it is the only way shattered lives can be healed. Gordon MacDonald said it so powerfully: "A broken world will never be rebuilt until we learn this principle of the unbound heart. It must be unwrapped and exposed to the light. The light will show some unattractive evil, but then something wonderful will happen. The love of God will be free to flood into the dark recesses and the rebuilding will begin. The Bible calls this unbinding process REPENTANCE." (*Rebuilding Your Broken World*, Thomas Nelson, Inc., 1988)

With Dr. Taylor's help, we both learned to ask, give, and receive forgiveness. I'm skeptical of any teaching that says forgiveness – asking, giving, or receiving – is quick and easy. This may work for minor offenses, but Ray and I were restoring a broken covenant, and it was a process that had to be done in layers. Of course, we both knew that God's forgiveness came quickly, freely, and fully. It was the receiving that took some time.

At the moment Ray revealed his sin to me, he asked immediately for forgiveness, but I was not prepared to give it. The trauma was too fresh, and I was unable to process the depth of pain and brokenness and could not (or would not) forgive. My first prayer concerning forgiveness was, "Oh, God! Please help me be willing to forgive." That was the best I could do at the time. But we learned to do something that would be deeply healing to our own hearts and rebuild the trust that was lost in our relationship. Ray learned to ask, and I learned to give forgiveness every time the pain and anger would rise between us. Layer upon layer, we were rebuilding broken places in our hearts and restoring trust in our marriage.

> **Prayer Point:** *Ask God to plant the seeds of His forgiveness in your heart. Be willing to let the seeds grow and flower in your life. Enjoy the beauty that results.*

Ray and I chose to locate in a city where we could live relatively hidden lives. We worked at secular jobs and, without other responsibilities, gave full attention to the work of rebuilding our lives from the inside out. God gave us a plan of action from Gordon MacDonald's *Rebuilding Your Broken World* that enabled us to navigate those difficult and often dark days.

First of all, Ray chose not to defend himself, but to acknowledge his guilt and responsibility. When a rumor surfaced or we learned of associates who freely spread the story of his failure, Ray remained silent. I often felt angry and defensive when these rumors reached my ears and wanted to tell the "real" story, but he urged me to let it go. Ray felt he deserved it all, but if any of it was undeserved, the Lord would be his defender.

We chose a church in our denomination to attend – a condition of the disciplinary process. The pastor, a gracious and loving friend for many years, welcomed us with kindness and understanding. Each Sunday, Ray and I slipped into the worship service just a couple of minutes late, found seats near the back, and exited quickly as the benediction was finished. We listened to the hymns, Scriptures, and every word of the sermon, hungering for hope. After church services, our time was spent alone, just the two of us, trying to find our way through this wilderness. Later, when we were restored to ministry, we looked at our congregation through different eyes, realizing that in every service there was someone with a broken heart who needed hope desperately.

> **Prayer Point:** *God, help me to offer hope to those who come seeking, not just the façade of the status quo, but your grace and mercy to a broken world in need of restoration.*

The path to restoration was long and painful, but we wanted no shortcuts. Ray's deep desire, as well as mine, was that the remainder of our days on earth be given fully to the One who redeemed us and to serving Him through ministry to a lost and broken world. A few days after Ray's sinful choice was made public, a dear and trusted friend gave us this passage from Luke 22:31-32 (NIV): "Simon, Simon, Satan has asked to sift you as wheat. But I have prayed for you, Simon, that your faith may not fail. And when you have turned back, strengthen your brothers." The turning back toward God was immediate, but the path to healing and wholeness took some time. This story is part of my response to "strengthen the [sisters]."

New patterns emerged in our lives. The Scriptures became precious and life-giving, not just material for sermons or teaching. We began to realize that we had value to God apart from our work for Him. He loved us simply because we belonged to Him. That understanding brought freedom to love others in a new way. We experienced a heightened sensitivity to the pain of others and a much less judgmental attitude. In a crowd, Ray and I found ourselves magnetically drawn to people who appeared broken and lonely.

Ray and I developed a more honest relationship with each other. Our commitment deepened, and the love that surfaced was like gold that had been tested in the fire, pure and strong. I no longer had illusions that Ray or I could not fail, so we guarded carefully any area that might be vulnerable to enemy attack. Ray was cautious about saying that he was "attacked by the enemy," lest he appear to shift the blame from himself. But it is true that any follower of Jesus is subject to enemy fire. With that understanding, we determined to expose any temptation to the light and never again be ignorant of Satan's schemes.

> ***Prayer Point:*** *Ask God to give you and your husband boldness to confront and expose temptation when it rears its head. Don't allow it to grow in hiding. Expose it to the light and disable it.*

Perhaps you are asking, "Will life ever be the same again?" I can only reply, "I hope not." This failure has marked us forever, and from time to time, we are reminded of the scars that are sometimes painful to the touch – the consequences of wrong choices. But the restoring power of grace given by God and by others has helped us find renewed meaning and purpose in life. Even after these many years, Ray feels awkward in large groups of his peers, always keenly aware that he hurt and disappointed so many.

Our unseen mentor, Gordon MacDonald, said, "The objective of rebuilding a broken world is not returning life to business-as-usual as if nothing had ever happened. That could never be. No, the objective is to come out of a dark time and finish the race with a depth of grace and humility that might not have happened under any other circumstances." Ray and I hate the sinful choice that brought such devastation to a thriving ministry and pain to our marriage, but we would never trade the lessons learned, the grace received, or the new life we now live.

Chariots of Fire has long been a favorite movie of ours. Eric Liddell, the son of a Scottish missionary and a gifted runner, was in the trials for Olympic track and field competition. His record up to these races was impressive, and his unorthodox form and intense passion had caught the attention of sportswriters all over Great Britain. Not many expected him to qualify for the Olympics, but Eric was an inspiration to watch. In one of the races, as Eric rounded a turn in the track, he was jostled into another runner and tumbled to the ground. With hundreds of people looking on, it appeared that all hope of qualifying was dashed. However, to the amazement of everyone, Eric stood up with blood and grime on his legs and elbows, got back on the track, and ran with all his heart. Arms flailing and head back in his own distinctive style, the "Flying Scotsman" not only qualified; he won the race! Ray's stumble brought both of us tumbling down, bruised and broken. But we looked closely at each other, helped one another back on the track, and thank God, we're still in the race.

The "W" Word

At the Death of a Spouse

by Melba E. Potter

The first time I called myself the "W" word, I was sitting with my mother in her living room, just a week after my husband's death. I spent the day with her – just the two of us – as much for her as for me. She had relied heavily on Mark's wisdom and insight, and she was hurting too. Daddy had been killed nine years prior. Mama had been 74 and married 50 years when she was thrown into the abyss of aloneness. I was 57 and married 35 years. Both of our husbands were vibrant, outgoing men of God who, without warning, faced sudden, grotesque ends – never to return.

On a Monday morning, February 29, my father was about to turn into the highway department to have his driver's license renewed when his car was struck from behind by a moving vehicle. His own car traveled forward about 70 feet and exploded in flames. Daddy went to heaven immediately from his "chariot of fire." I couldn't believe how she managed, but my mother was amazing. I was to learn her source of strength nine years later.

My husband, Mark, had gotten what he wanted for Christmas – total cooperation from our entire immediate family. All were present for the day – lots of good food and presents. He took the boys out back to shoot skeet, and then we all traveled the 30 miles to my mom's house, a tradition. More good food, gifts, reunion with more family, singing, and then we all began the bundling up of children and leaving. We left to go to our oldest son's home to see the two little girls' "Christmas." About an hour passed, and Mark stood up and said, "It's time to go home." Amid disagreeing protests of

"Nooo, Pa-Pa, stay," he said further, "No, we've had a great day, but everybody's tired, and we need to go home."

It was after dark, so he naturally reached for my keys. We got into my car, a 1994 midnight blue Explorer. My daughter-in-law kissed his nearly bald head, pinched his cheek, and handed the seat belt to him. We drove off, and within five minutes he was "home." We had been hit by a speeding motorcycle on his side of the car. Both the cyclist and Mark died in a moment of terrible noise, shattered glass, and the horrible realization that my husband was with the Lord.

That night, when I was allowed to leave the hospital, I needed to see my mother. She understood what I was going through, and I knew what she was thinking. Needless to say, Mama and I had much to share. I needed to learn how she did it, for now we were both widows.

In retrospect, my vision has become clearer, and I now see how God was leading me then, has led me this far, and will lead on into the future. There are several principles I've learned from experience and observation through the seasons of life. I believe God will guide anyone who will allow himself to be led.

Preparation

Before marriage, you must prepare by learning all you can about each other, likes and dislikes, families, and peculiarities. The wedding is planned, and the days following are full of wonderfully new information. You continue on, blissfully aware of each other, never believing anything could ever spoil these idyllic days. Along come the first argument, children, and financial distress ... troubles come.

Understand this statistic: over 75 percent of women will be widowed. Knowing this should be the impetus to discover everything possible about the business of your family. Where are the important documents? When are the bills to be paid? What financial investments will be considered? On what dates are the household bills due? Have we made wills?

Needing to know all this information is not a lack of trust in your husband's ability to care for you. When your spouse dies, the numbers don't stop. The world goes on, and they expect their money. Talk now, together. Knowledge is power, and this power gives confidence. Although nothing can erase the initial acute despair of loss, having walked through your vital financial plans will ease many a worried moment in the weeks and months following the death of your spouse. Begin now to honor him in this manner. "So teach us to number our days that we may apply our hearts unto wisdom" (Psalm 90:12).

Acceptance

It has happened. Half of your self – body, soul, and spirit – is gone. Permanently. No reversal. Life as you knew it has changed forever. There may be a period of denial before you can accept it fully, but he won't come up the steps into the back door again. Ever. But God and His Holy Spirit are very present, almost tangibly. He is nearer to you now than ever before. "Thy Maker is thine husband; the Lord of hosts is his name ..." (Isaiah 54:5).

I began to feel very early in my widowhood that I was my Father's very special child – that it certainly was sad for everybody else that He just loved me best! There were times when I felt I was walking a few inches off the ground – I felt cushioned on all sides by the very shield of the Holy Spirit. Oh, I felt very protected.

Begin to give your adoration to Him. Tell Him how much you love Him because He will return your affection. He has always loved you; you simply feel it more now. God has allowed this temporary separation, and you are still here by His design and purpose. Lean hard against Him. Let Him breathe His life and strength into you that you may overcome. "... He who began a good work in you will carry it on to completion until the day of Christ Jesus" (Philippians 1:6). Your "becoming" will not be stunted. Wait, trust, and see!

Grieving

Yes! Do...as long as it takes. Giving vent to your sorrow is as necessary as breathing. Healing cannot occur unless you do. Listen to your own heart and mind, and observe your loss in whatever means fits you. God made the individual ... you are like no other.

Grief is not measured by outward signs and emotions. In fact, it cannot be measured. There is no gauge – no standard – because it is so personal. It is present every moment in your personal pain, and every memory is a fresh wound. The deepest, most healing aspect of your grief must be dealt with by you alone. People may surround you, but your way must be walked alone for its destination to be reached. Getting mired in the "what ifs" is a possibility – What if we had waited? What if I hadn't done this? What if someone had not needed him? No! No! No! What has happened cannot be changed. Guilt may be overwhelming because you remain and he is dead. Do not allow moments immediately prior – perhaps words said in haste – to supersede a lifetime of dear remembrance. This has not been done to you. It was an act God allowed. "He will keep you in perfect peace as you trust Him" (Isaiah 26:3, paraphrased).

Acknowledge God

There are many promises in God's word with your name on them!

He is Faithful – 1 Corinthians 10:13

He has a plan for you – Jeremiah 29:11

He guides you continually – Philippians 1:6

He knows the needs of the widow – Psalm 68:5
    and 72:12; James 1:27

You will not be alone – Deuteronomy 31:6;
Psalm 94:14

These are only a few. Read on and on.

As you acknowledge God's concern for the details of your life, the praises will flow. As you praise Him in these details every day, you will see how much He loves you. He loves your praise, and it pleases Him when you praise Him.

Adjusting

Listen closely. This is not a new chapter in your life. It is an entirely new volume. All that was written before is merely an introduction to the fulfillment God had planned for you in the beginning. You can't just "pick up" and go on, but as you learn a new plane of trust, you will be led slowly, deliberately out of the darkness and confusion that seems now to surround you. Take your time. Don't rush. The pain that is in every thought will dull. Get counsel from an objective, trustworthy source. Allow your dear ones to carry you. Talk to those whom you know will be faithful with your words and thoughts and keep them safely. Older, mature widows will delight in your confidence. Their wisdom will strengthen you. Throughout these days, I've found Ecclesiastes 3 is true.

New Relationships

Because of this new experience, God will lead you into new relationships involving those whom you never would have met. New friendships will be formed, and new employment of your giftings will amaze you. Those who were just acquaintances may come into your circle of friends. Allow yourself to enjoy these treasures. You'll be better, your life richer as you step into this stream. Begin to step out of yourself into a new activity or ministry. An aura of beauty that comes only from intense suffering will surround you. God will be honored by your behavior as you give yourself to your friends. "A friend loveth at all times, and a brother is born for adversity" (Proverbs 17:17). One who has friends must show himself a friend, and "there is a friend who sticks closer than a brother" (Proverbs 18:24, NIV).

Acknowledge your Personhood

You were unique the moment you were born. Special to God, you were formed from traits, gifts, and chemistry of generations. Your first family welcomed you, and they began to observe your development into what God had ordained. Suddenly, now you've hit a wall. If you remain in this place, you'll die in every way. If you choose to allow your roots to grow into the rich loam of all that you've known to be true, you'll see who God is and that His ways are perfect. You'll know His plans for you are better than you imagined! You are His treasure, and He's still polishing you. You're here, and God is forever. "He knows the way that I take: when He has tried me, I shall come forth as gold" (Job 23:10).

Shortly after my husband died, someone sent me this beautiful prayer written by an unknown author. It was a comfort, and I now use it in ministry to others:

At the Death of Husband
Thank you, Father,
for giving us as much time together as we had.
Spare me now from further pain of self-pity.
I accept the fact that I have no right to expect
that I can be so highly privileged
as to never taste sorrow in my lifetime.
This is my time to experience a cross, and I do so bravely.
I remember with joy and gratitude our wedding day.
You made no promises to us then,
guaranteeing a fixed number of years together.
I thank you for what we have had,
and I will not think about what we could have had.

96

I will look now at what I have left,
not at what I have lost.
I thank you, Father, that there was
no ignoble scene of angry parting,
only the honored call of God
who has glorified our marriage with the call of eternity.
My tears are tears of love and gratitude.
I thank you that our love for each other is still alive.
I sense that I am surrounded by an invisible
presence and power of an indescribable love.
It is the comfort of your Spirit.
I praise you, God and Father, for your goodness.
I have tasted grief,
But I will not have wasted this grief.
Make me into a softer, gentler soul!
Amen.

I bless God for my husband. His love and faithfulness to me still make me strong. Who he was will be with me always. My family – sisters, children, grandchildren – were my strength. They carried me until I could go on alone. In their pain, they mothered me. I thank God for my own mother, who showed me by her example. She was my rock. I praise God for bringing me from fear to faith into a higher place in Him. "He has made the valley of misery into a well" (Psalm 84:6, paraphrased).

SUCCESSES

- ***My Priceless Heritage***

- ***Destiny Beating in Our Hearts***

- ***Staying Power***

- ***Give Me a Break***

- ***My Guided Life***

My Priceless Heritage

Reflections of a Grateful Preacher's Kid

by Emily Wood Jackson

There it was ... one last flash, the extra flash from the rear of Dad's car. He gave the brakes a tap or two just for us as he pulled away from the house, drove down the big hill, and vanished onto the highway. It was a small reminder that he knew we were watching, and we loved knowing he was still thinking of us. It was like another hug from Dad, and I needed that as I wiped away a few more tears. He was off again for ministry. Mom warmly got my three siblings and me distracted with other tasks. Edwina practiced for her piano lesson, Eddie went back to playing ball, and Elaine and I returned to our dolls. We kept busy until it was time for bedtime prayers and perhaps a call from Dad.

As a minister, my dad lived according to his sense of calling to serve the Lord. He had been a pastor for 13 years before he became the conference Christian Education director. Now his responsibilities required that he travel a great deal. Even though his absence was always hard for us, we understood it to be part of God's plan. God was his guide, and we were taught that God's guidance is always best. It was easier for us to let him go because we knew he was going to serve the Lord. He and Mom lived a life of commitment and dedication before us. Our first lesson about what it meant to be a disciple didn't come from Sunday school; it came from my parents. They knew who they were in Christ, and they lived it at church as well as at home.

They taught us how important it was to have an identity like that too. In our earliest memories, we were taught to know who we could be in Christ. We were always learning the Truth of God's Word and the importance of loving Jesus daily. We understood that we could choose Jesus as our Savior and have a personal relationship with Him. My siblings and I love our parents dearly for teaching us this Truth consistently with the life they model.

One way that Mom and Dad made sure we learned this most important lesson was to see that we had a church we could call home. My early childhood years corresponded with the 14 years that Dad served as Christian Education director for the Appalachian Conference of the International Pentecostal Holiness Church. When I remember those emotional departure scenes, it seems it would have been far easier to join Dad for his journeys. Whether the trip was to be short or long, there were usually tears involved. It just wasn't easy to see him go. We loved our father and hated not having him at home. Obviously, the calendar would not always allow for us even to think of going. Dad's trips often involved several days. However, when the travel would be only for a weekend, many thought it would just make sense for us to join Dad. In fact, that is what he first thought. Dad remembers when Mom told him of her concerns and how together they decided that their children would not just travel with him to attend church everywhere. Rather, we would always know a "home church" and be very involved there. We would have a sense of belonging to a church family. While the teary good-byes never got easier nor fully disappeared, we came to value that wise choice of our parents.

Growing up with a church home gave us a sense of identity and responsibility in the Body of Christ. It would seem to some that we were at church all the time. I suppose in many ways we were! Whether it was regular service time or a special activity, if it were at all possible, we were going to participate. We were taught that such participation was not an obligation but an opportunity to learn more about Jesus, serve Him, and use our talents for His glory. It was never a requirement because we were preacher's kids. Rather, it was a matter of obedience as a believer. The Church is Christ's Body (Ephesians 1:23), and we were to be active in it to fulfill God's plan for the advancement of His kingdom.

Mom and Dad didn't take a casual approach to our church involvement. They helped to lead us in our interests with careful support and also by example. They didn't merely send us to Bible Quiz practice; Mom coached the team. They didn't only tell us the importance of using our talents for God; our parents made sure we participated in the Talent Program each year. How many car washes and bake sales did they endure, and how many candy bars did they sell for our youth group's fund-raisers? Mom and Dad made the church family part of our own family, and we desired to be involved.

Children incessantly learn from their parents' choices, and we were no exception. Whether it was praying, studying the Bible, visiting those in need, or providing fun evenings for the youth, we observed our parents being faithful in their personal commitment to Christ. As soon as we were each old enough, we accepted responsibilities too. While I was still attending children's church, Edwina was already helping to teach. Each of us naturally grew up into God's service, and that pattern has continued throughout the years.

Participating in the local church taught us about ministry and helped us understand our parents' dedication to serving God. It was important for us to realize where Dad had been and what he was doing for God's kingdom. Perhaps we did not always truly understand the full nature of a particular event, but we were occasionally given the opportunity to go with Dad on his ministry trips. We nearly always participated in some way.

In some ministers' homes, ministry is perceived as an interruption to the family. In our home, Mom and Dad carried out their calling with joy and taught us that we could take part in what our dad was doing. With Edwina accompanying us on the piano, Eddie, Elaine, and I would often sing songs for the service. We couldn't claim that it always went perfectly – some churches where we sang would say an "Amen!" to that – but the idea was to be a part of the ministry. We were working together for the kingdom of God, and all had a role to play to accomplish His purposes.

One valuable way my siblings and I learned to function in our own identities in Christ was through prayer. At a very young age, I became aware of the important role prayer should play in the life of a believer. It was just another busy school morning at the Wood house, or at least I thought so. I had not even begun school yet and was enjoying pre-kindergarten days at home. Once they had everything together, Dad headed out the door with Edwina, Eddie, and Elaine to taxi them to school. As soon as they were gone, Mom called for me to come into the room where she was. "We must say a prayer, Emily. Your dad has lost a special book. He cannot find his date book, and it is very important that he find it," Mom told me. So we prayed. It was just that simple. Mom and I bowed our heads and asked God to help us find Dad's book.

Being only four years old, I could not possibly understand the worry that was caused by a missing date book. This was long before the days of Palm Pilots or a saved computer copy at the office. If Dad had lost his date book, he was going to have trouble for the year. But with the simplicity of a child's thinking, all I knew was that there was a problem, and we needed to pray.

Just a few hours after our prayer, the telephone rang. It was someone at the local pharmacy letting us know that Dad's date book had been found in their parking lot. Mom's face beamed with relief and joy as she quickly called Dad to let him know. When she shared the story, she told him that we had prayed and that God had answered our prayer. Even though it may seem quite simple, that experience taught me a great lesson. As God's child, I can know He hears and answers my prayers. Regardless of the nature of the problem, God cares.

The value of prayer was taught daily through experience. Whether it was for our own needs or the needs of others, we were to talk to God continually (1 Thessalonians 5:17). With the mind-set of knowing that He was in control, we could trust Him in all circumstances and give Him thanks (1 Thessalonians 5:18). We prayed together as a family and were encouraged to pray in our own personal time as well. Wherever we were, God would hear us and in His wisdom, meet our needs.

On the night when we got the call that Mom had been in a car accident and had a head-on collision with a bus, I am thankful that we already knew the power of prayer. Even though we did not know the severity of Mom's injuries or the likelihood of her recovery, we knew without any doubt that God would hear our prayer. We could trust that He would take care of Mom. While the next months were challenging, God heard us and answered our many requests for complete health. On tough days and pleasant ones, we knew God was listening, and we could give all of our cares to Him because He cares for us (1 Peter 5:7).

> **Prayer Point:** *Help us as parents not only to speak in public about the importance of prayer, but also to model the importance and power of prayer daily in our personal lives.*

Not only did we participate in prayer together, but we also participated in the practice of giving. We knew that we were to give of our time and talents, but Mom and Dad also taught us to give of our finances for God's work. Very early, we understood that all our provision and blessings came from God. It was our privilege to give back to God for His purposes. Whether it was giving tithe from money earned babysitting or mowing a lawn, pledging to support a missionary, or participating in the general offering, we found the joy that was gained by doing so. We saw our parents giving and could follow their example. They desired to give as freely as they had received (Matthew 10:7). As children, we were aware of the missionaries they supported and understood the need for coupling monetary gifts with continual prayer. We not only learned to believe in the sustained financial support of missions, but we also learned the value of giving our time to participate in short-term missions work ourselves.

In teaching us this beautiful cycle of giving back to our heavenly Father, who has blessed us, we also learned to depend on God's provision. As far as money matters were concerned, we children never really knew details. Mom and Dad made us aware of God's provision, not of any financial challenges they faced. We now realize that some seasons must have been difficult. We have known many preachers' kids who were often complaining about money and felt resentment toward the church. When we reflect on our parents' choice, we are glad that they protected our mind-sets when it came to knowing such matters. We didn't have issues with individuals or boards; rather, we knew our needs were met.

Because Mom and Dad knew the value of experience and the influence it would make on our lives, we were active in more than the life of the local congregation. They enabled us to see the larger picture of what was happening in the denomination as a whole. My parents gave priority to making it possible for all four of us kids to have the opportunity to attend events like General Conferences and Christian Education Conferences. We realized that many adults made other arrangements for their children and did not bring them along to such events. It definitely would have been easier to leave the kids behind and take a quick flight. Instead, our whole family would load up and head off for the adventure. We stopped for picnics along the way, and we played creative games to keep our minds off the monotony of travel and the tight arrangements. Between another round of singing "Everybody Ought to Go to Sunday

School" and the countless inquiries of "How much farther?" Mom and Dad must have grown tired of those long trips. Nonetheless, they made them time and again and created lifelong memories for us.

Once we finally arrived at our destination, it wasn't always comfortable. Typically, there was a rotation from night to night of who would get the bed or one of the sleeping bags. We have funny memories of those days together and enjoy lots of laughs when we remember trying to make room for one another and not trip over someone's head on the way to the bathroom in the middle of the night. My siblings and I are left appreciating the patience my parents displayed in such times and absolutely admiring their willingness to make the necessary sacrifices to have us with them.

There were many experiences we were introduced to through our times with the general church. Not only did we remember the children's activities that were provided, but we also got to meet missionaries, college representatives, pastors, and plenty of other people from different areas of ministry. Regardless of the exact event, the goal was achieved. We got a glimpse of the larger church, and it broadened our view of what God was doing all over the world. Moreover, we also developed friendships with other Christians and learned about growing in the Lord together.

As thankful as we were for a church family, we were keenly aware that our own family took precedence. Mom and Dad let us know that nothing they did was more important to them than us. I can't count the number of times when I have heard of homes that have been ruined because a minister loved the church more than his own family. It is possible to busy ourselves so much with our tasks that we forget our purpose! Loving God doesn't start in the public arena; it starts in the home. Mom and Dad were careful to do exactly that. My siblings and I never doubted that we were priority. We always felt that we were our parents' main concern.

They did their best to make us a normal family. We were not "different" because we were preacher's kids. We didn't have to live up to the infamous double standard. We were normal children with all that goes along with that. When we didn't make the best choices, Mom and Dad provided corrective discipline to keep us focused on following God's standards rather than people's expectations.

> ***Prayer Point:*** *Ask God to give your children a love for His Word, as well as an understanding of the special calling on your lives. Pray that the seed of resentment will not find fertile soil in your child's life.*

Family time together was a jewel for us, and we cherished it. Whether it was a regular evening meal or a summer vacation, we knew that we would share time together and could count on one another for anything. Mom and Dad made time for asking questions and learning about everything that was happening in our lives. In the busiest seasons on the church calendar, there was always time for us too. From general questions after a regular day of school to the phone call after our first days in college, their being interested in our daily lives gave us a sense of accountability and a reminder of their love.

Like many preachers' kids, it is true that we lived in what some consider a "glass house." Many people were quite interested in our lives and sometimes seemed to be "inspecting" us. We realized that others were noticing how we lived and what choices we made. We viewed that fact as a constant opportunity to let others know about Christ. We were not "ashamed of the gospel because it is the power of God for the salvation of everyone who believes" (Romans 1:16). We knew that others were watching and realized how easily our witness could be ruined by thoughtless actions (Proverbs 22:1).

> ***Prayer Point:*** *Father, when my children look back on their years in a ministry family, I pray that their memories will not be of the inconvenient or uncomfortable by-products of ministry life, but of the tremendous heritage they are blessed to have.*

Occasionally, we would feel that others were far too interested in us. We were encouraged to view these people as "curious" rather than "nosy." It was challenging to overlook at times. While Mom and Dad could try to keep us in a right attitude about things, they simply could not control others. Rather than making us feel as though we were on display in our "glass house," Mom and Dad simply "pulled the blinds." They set boundaries with regard to what would be shared with others. They would not use our personal stories as illustrations, and we could trust them fully with personal concerns. We knew that our family business was ours alone. Naturally, we were not living in a vacuum. We were affected by the world around us. However, Mom and Dad's prioritizing our privacy secured our feelings of trust in them as our parents. We had a sense that our house was our family's home even when we shared it with traveling evangelists, missionaries, or other guests.

Privacy went the other direction too. People's problems and struggles were not discussions at our dinner table. Moreover, Mom and Dad did not make issues at church the focus of home discussions. In this way, the problems of others did not color our perception of God's work or of His people. Sometimes, preachers' kids are too familiar with the troubles of the church and become embittered by seeing only negative things. There can be so much focus on the problems that the good is often forgotten. Mom and Dad made certain that was not our experience. Instead, when we were young, we simply weren't aware of such issues. As we grew older and naturally realized that these things were happening, they were addressed only for purposes of prayer, not for chats over dinner. "Judge not that ye be not judged" was an instant remedy to the temptation to talk about others (Matthew 7:1).

Like most preachers' families, we had to move as my dad's position changed. We were certainly not immune to the challenges that come with transition. New friends had to be found, new schools attended, and a new parsonage had to be made home. After his time as conference C.E. director, Dad pastored a local congregation for four more years, served as conference superintendent for 11 years, and then became the Stewardship Ministries director in Oklahoma, where he is presently serving. During each move, it was vitally important for us to remember that our omniscient God is in full control. There are simply no surprises for Him. We may not know the details of the next destination, but He does.

These truths guided Edwina, Eddie, Elaine, and me when it came time for us to make our decisions about going to college. Mom and Dad advised us early on the importance of seeking God's guidance. We had witnessed their faith during times of change and followed their example in prayerfully seeking the Holy Spirit's direction. While some pastors made financial support of their children contingent upon their children's specific choices, Mom and Dad made it clear that they would support our choice of schools wherever we felt was God's will. We each prayerfully chose to attend Emmanuel College and are grateful for the influence those years had on our lives.

Because Mom and Dad allowed us to make our own decisions, we had the personal peace that God provided in leading us there. Our parents supported us with their prayers and were faithful to continue to support our participation in ministry. We can't count the number of times we saw Edwina in the Emmanuel Players' presentation of "Simon the Leper" or heard an Emmanuel Singers concert with Eddie, Elaine, or me. Those years continued to teach each of us about serving the Lord while we enjoyed learning and growing within a circle of strong Christian friends.

Today, each of us is serving God in different areas. In North Carolina, Edwina assists with the children's ministry in Winston-Salem, and Eddie is an associate pastor at Northwood Temple in Fayetteville. Elaine is a children's pastor at the Radford Worship Center in Virginia. After also being involved in ministry at Northwood Temple, I am now living in Germany with my husband, who is a pastor and is studying for future years of ministry. Regardless of the miles between us, my family remains very close as we value the role we each have within the Body of Christ. We still know those moments of teary departures, but we find joy in knowing we are at home wherever we find ourselves doing His will.

Our lives as preacher's kids have been blessed abundantly. As Eddie and Freda Wood's children, we were raised to love Christ. Our spiritual heritage is more valuable than any material thing we could ever own. We treasure the memories of our childhood days and the wonderful life we have known as we continue to grow in Christ. We are a preacher's kids, but Mom and Dad taught us first to prize the great love our heavenly "Father has lavished on us, that we should be called children of God..." (1 John 3:1, NIV).

Destiny Beating in Our Hearts

The Down and Up Life of a Church Planter's Wife

by Hope Carpenter

My role as the wife of a church planter ...Wow! How do I begin? The last 15 years have been the most wonderfully exciting yet difficult and eye-opening years of my life.

I met Ron Carpenter, Jr., in 1987 at Emmanuel College. I was a freshman, and he was a sophomore who had already entered the School of Christian Ministries and was well on his way to becoming a "preacher." It really was love at first sight. I saw him and knew that my destiny was all wrapped up in that tall, handsome, blond guy known as Ron, Jr.

I came from a small town, Calhoun Falls, South Carolina, where I was a little Baptist girl until my parents were filled with the Holy Spirit. Soon after, we were given the right *foot* of Christian fellowship (a nice way of saying we were kicked out). We then went to the Pentecostal Holiness Church and thought we had died and gone to heaven. My parents were so hungry for God. You see, we weren't raised in Pentecost, and therefore we didn't take it for granted. They dragged me to every revival, tent meeting, Full Gospel Business Men's meetings, and Kenneth Copeland Crusade they could find. I received the baptism of the Holy Spirit when I was 12 in one of those revivals. That was it ... I was hooked. I loved the Lord with all my heart and knew that I had a powerful call on my life. My mother always told me I would marry a preacher one day. Thank God for parents who can hear the voice of God and point you in the direction that you should go.

Ron and I were married June 23, 1990, and immediately moved to Knoxville, Tennessee, to help plant a church.

We were interns, meaning basically that we did all the stuff nobody wants to do but that has to be done. We took out the trash, set up the sound equipment for each service, took *down* the sound equipment, set up the nursery, took *down* the nursery, made phone calls, picked up the church people and took them home, led praise and worship, and even had to keep the keyboard in the backseat of our car when we weren't having service or practicing! We were newlyweds, in a foreign city, with no friends or family, and with no money because we lived on whatever came in that month; and I was in school full-time trying to finish my second degree. If that isn't a train wreck waiting to happen, I don't know what is.

All this time, we had destiny beating in our hearts. We just knew God was going to do something powerful through us, but we continued to "take out the trash." God was teaching us principles of servanthood and spiritual authority, and we didn't even know it. Jesus said that if you are faithful in little, He will reward you with much (Matthew 25:23). We had only three voices on our praise team – two of them being Ron and me. We had only a keyboard and a trumpet, but we practiced every week, and we gave God the biggest and best praise that we knew how to give Him. We were on time. As a matter of fact, we were usually the first ones there!

We went to Knoxville with big dreams and goals, but we found out early in the church plant that Knoxville was boot camp for us, not our ultimate destiny. We were there for 10 months when God opened the door for us to move to Greenville, South Carolina, to plant a church with the help of the Pentecostal Holiness Church. I'll never forget the day we were loading our U-Haul truck and moving from our little apartment (our castle), feeling like such failures. We went there to build a powerful church, but God wanted us there to "make" us. God cannot fill what He hasn't formed. We were young and zealous for God, but we left broken and empty – just the right combination for God to start building us and filling us.

Prayer Point: *Am I willing for God to form me into a vessel He can fill?*

We arrived in Greenville with no place to live, no money, no core group of people to start with, no musicians, no building ... just two broken people who were crazy enough to start over and try again. We didn't know all the ins and outs of church planting. We didn't have a mentor. We hadn't been to mega-ministries with successful stories. We loved God with all our hearts, we loved each other, and we loved people. All we wanted to do was to love people and show them that Jesus is the answer to any problem they have.

We lived with Ron's parents for several months until we could find a place of our own. We were just so thankful to have *meals* to eat! We had lived on bologna sandwiches and Kool-Aid for the last year in Knoxville. In those first few months in Greenville, we regrouped as a couple, got our confidence back, and struck out again to do something powerful for God.

We named the church (membership: 2) Redemption Outreach Center because that had been the story of our lives – redemption – and we wanted to take redemption "out" to the world. Several years later, God told us to change our name to Redemption World Outreach Center, because we would eventually reach the world with the Gospel. Man, we looked stupid doing that when we had only several hundred people, but faith calls things that are not as though they are (Romans 4:17). We had to call it what God saw long before it ever became a world outreach center.

We had enough sense to know that we didn't want to go after "church people," so we went to any drunk on the street, cashier at the Quick Stop, waiter at the Pizza Hut, neighbor at our apartment, and the few people that we already knew in Greenville. We had only a few months to find a building, organize, invite, and get ready for our opening service on August 19, 1991. Our opening day, we had 73 people show up, mostly family, conference officials, and the few drunks we picked up on the way ourselves. We greeted people at the door, welcomed them from the pulpit (a music stand), led worship, took up the offering, preached, and taught children's church. We were a two-man band. I had a girlfriend from college who came and helped us with the nursery for two months, and that's really the only help we had.

Ron had told his former roommate from Emmanuel College, Sam Shelton, that if we ever had a church, he wanted Sam to come and lead worship for us. Unfortunately, having no money, we couldn't pay him to come. We got brave and asked him to come down on the weekends for $25 a week. It was stretching our faith to commit a whopping $25 a week! He stayed with us in our apartment, and thus began our journey together. Ron and Sam are as different as night and day, but they linked themselves in the spirit the year that they were roommates. They prayed together every day, studied the Word, and grew in God. They worshiped together in that little dorm room, not knowing that they were pouring the foundation, in those days, for the stage that they minister from today. The things that we do in quiet, God rewards openly (Matthew 6:6).

We were now in Greenville, with a small little church of about 40 on a good day and 25 usually. I enrolled in the University of South Carolina at Spartanburg trying desperately to finish my degree, a task that would take another two years. We worked hard trying to grow the church, one desperate family at a time. We had every reject, convict, and flimflammer there was.

Ron played the drums until our first drummer joined the church. We found him walking the streets drunk. We found him a job and an apartment, and we blessed him and his wife with a housewarming shower, only to find out later, during a powerful service we had, that they felt really convicted about living together since they were both married to other people and hadn't gotten divorced yet! That is the story of our ministry. We reach out with God's redeeming love and liberating power to those whom most people wouldn't have in their churches, and we pour our lives into them until their revelation changes their situation.

> **Prayer Point:** *Do I have the patience to carry on with the work I've been given, with the people I have around me?*

Our lives will always parallel our revelation. A good heart is not enough. The right heart but the wrong head will never prosper. The Bible says that we, our minds, are renewed, transformed, daily, that we may be able to prove what is that good and acceptable and perfect will of God (Romans 12:2). We can't walk out the will of God until we have gotten our minds transformed by the Word, which is also a daily process. *It takes time.*

We spent many long days and nights pouring into the people God brought us. Some would stay and change; others would give up and go back to their old way of life. We never gave people "false hope" that when they accepted Christ, tulips would pop up all over their lives. Rather, they were in for the fight of their lives. Some were willing to be processed, and others were not.

It's the same today with over 7,000 members. We have probably lost over 20,000 people, but the 7,000 we have are very aware of the process. Nothing happens overnight, and freedom is never free. There has always been and there will always be a price for freedom. This principle really hit home for us shortly after we started our church.

When Ron and I met, we were the Ken and Barbie of Emmanuel College: Mr. Everything and Miss Emmanuel. We both had a past, but neither one of us knew it. I was raped on a date when I was 15 years old, and that led me down the road of alcohol and promiscuity. I ended up at an altar a very messed-up 18-year-old little girl. I thought coming clean with God would make it all "go away." It didn't. I thought being a good Christian, good wife, good pastor's wife, would get all the junk out, but it didn't.

Ron had a past of partying and pornography, and he thought that the salvation experience would make all those desires just "go away." Once again, it didn't. We were hiding behind all our church planting, pastoring, and son-of-the-superintendent masks. We had secrets from each other, and we had a constant battle in our minds for freedom. It didn't take long to realize that to help others, we must come clean and pursue freedom for ourselves.

> **Prayer Point:** *God, open my heart to any hidden thing that might hinder my relationship with you, and my effectiveness in your kingdom.*

I went to the altar and begged God to heal me time and time again. I still got up with a poor self-image, low self-esteem, and the inability to give myself to my husband and others in the way God desired for my life. I thought that God would heal me instantly – poof, all gone! It wasn't until three years later, when I was pregnant with our second child, that I began to understand the process of freedom.

I started a Bible study called *Woman, Thou Art Loosed* by T. D. Jakes, and that study opened my eyes to the fact that I must pursue freedom; freedom doesn't pursue me. Jesus has already done all He is going to do to heal me. He doesn't have to heal me all over again; rather, I must align myself with His principles of healing. I had to bathe myself in the Word on a level that I had never done before. I had to be pressed and processed, and that was a painful time. Just because God had forgiven me and didn't remember it anymore didn't mean I had forgiven myself and didn't remember it anymore.

I was in the fight of my life to uproot the old junk and plant new seeds of God's Word in my mind to overcome my issues. It was a slow, grueling process, but I stand confident today, knowing who I am in Christ and what He has done for me. My life is now a testimony of hope, restoration, grace, and freedom. That is why I am so passionate to see people's lives changed and transformed to the fullest. I don't believe in settling for second best and mediocrity. Once you've really tasted freedom, you can't go back to wearing masks and faking your way through another church service. The prize is so worth the process.

After I had graduated, finally, in 1993, I found out I was pregnant with our first son, Chase. I tell people, as I describe Chase, that he is like the very best and the very worst of both Ron and me, all wrapped up in one child. He is like the Energizer bunny on speed! We have since discovered that he has ADHD (attention deficit disorder with hyperactivity), and once again, the process of God is at work *in us!*

We were at war within ourselves over whether to medicate him. You see, we are of the persuasion that God can heal anything and that the Blood has never lost and will never lose its power. Well, we prayed, fasted, anointed, bound, rebuked, cried, and cast out, and it only got worse. He was doing poorly in school and dominating every person in his life – not the recipe for success. When will we ever learn? His ways are not our ways, His thoughts are not our thoughts, and they are much higher than ours (Isaiah 55:8-9).

During this trying time in my life as a mother, I asked the Lord, just as King David did, "Show me *your* ways, O Lord; teach me *your* paths" (Psalm 25:4). I have learned over the years that God is very concerned with what is concerning me, and He has the answers if I will just ask him and pursue Him. I wanted immediate deliverance for my son; God required us to walk through it to teach us about His sovereignty.

Look at the children of Israel. They looked at the Red Sea and said, "Surely not." Evidently, they needed to walk through it! Look at the fiery furnace. God could have walked out of the fire, but no, He required them to walk into the fire to show off His power! Praise His name! Naaman, the leper, had the faith that he could be healed, but when Elijah told him to go dip seven times in the muddy river to get healed, he almost forfeited his healing because of the *method* God chose to use.

Have we given up on the fact that Jesus can heal Chase? No! It's in His time and in His way. We still confess daily that our children have the mind of Christ and that every chemical in their bodies must line up with the Word of God, and we speak "peace" to them, declaring *"nothing missing, nothing broken."*

During this time, I was teaching music in our home to help makes ends meet so that Ron wouldn't have to work a secular job and could focus all his attention on building the church. I typed the bulletin, continued to teach children's church, and filled any other gaps that we might have. Even though I was still a very broken and insecure young woman, I worked as hard as I could to do whatever needed to be done. I would pray for and minister to women day after day for them to be healed, and I needed healing myself. It would have been much easier to remain a "victim" and wallow in my own issues and withdraw from the ministry. It was much more difficult to minister out of my pain.

> ***Prayer Point:*** *Lord, work in me as I strive to be the partner and helper my husband needs during this process. Teach me to work through my issues instead of taking the easy road.*

We went on to have two more children, Chaz and Chanlin Praise, and two of the three with no insurance. That's a whole other story, a whole other book! We have been through many problems planting this church. Nothing has been easy. We've been lied about, talked about, misunderstood, and made fun of, but none of it has stopped us. There have been so many times we would lie in our bed and sob tears from hurt, rejection, words, and looks, but we knew in our hearts that God had called us, He had anointed us, and we were doing exactly what *He* wanted us to do.

We had to decide early on whether we wanted to be popular or powerful. We have found that if you step out to do anything powerful for God, out of the ordinary, you will be a target for criticism. Why? Exceptional always violates ordinary. There is a huge price to pay, and not many are willing to pay it.

What is my role as the wife of a church planter? Be a great Christian. I have worked in every ministry there is. I cooked hotdogs for our outreach programs when it was only Ron and me, long before we had all the buses and the nice facilities. I cleaned bathrooms, babies' booties, snotty noses, and even single moms' houses just to be a blessing to them. I've cooked pots of spaghetti and visited sick people long before we ever had a "visitation ministry." I personally called all the visitors every week for at least five years. And at the same time, I was a mother of three in less than four years, finished two degrees, kept house, cooked dinner, never neglected my husband, and became a strong, independent, on-fire woman of God.

How do I do it all? People ask me that almost every day. I don't. It's Christ in me. I don't operate in my own strength; I can't operate in my own strength. The task is too large, too hard, and too heavy. I traded my burden a long time ago, when I got the revelation that I had to pursue Him. His yoke is easy, and His burden is so light (Matthew 11:30).

I know who I am in Christ now, and I choose to walk in it. If God says I can have it, no one can take it from me. If God says I can be it, no one can convince me differently. If God says I can do it, hell can't keep me from it. It is a mandate from God to all of us to give out freely what He has so freely given to us (Matthew 10:8). The Kingdom of Heaven is healing the sick, cleansing the lepers, raising the dead, and casting out demons; and Jesus said clearly in that passage that just as you've received these things, you should give them out.

People ask us all the time, "How'd you do it?" They want us to give them the formula for building a big church, the formula for being successful. I don't believe there is a set formula, or 10 steps to church planting, or a conference you can attend to give you the hidden recipe for success. Our only answer is this: We just loved people, and we just love God with our whole hearts. Whatever He has done for us, we have been willing, no matter how hard it was, to be the vessels that His healing, cleansing, raising, casting out, and love can flow through.

People look at us today and see the big church, the nice cars, and the nice home, and they want what we have *right now*. What they don't see is the *process* – what it took to be pressed, built, and "made." God is not concerned with building great ministries. God is concerned with building great people. Ron and I started long ago with destiny in our hearts; and together, we were willing to do whatever it took to meet the needs of the people and to please God with our lives.

It sounds too simple, I know, just to love the Lord with all your heart, soul, mind, and strength, and then to love others just like that too. It sounds simple, but it's the challenge Jesus came with, a very difficult one (Matthew 22:34-40). That has been the driving force in our lives: to love that way.

Love is what built our ministry, our marriage, and our lives. God so radically reached down to the unlovable – me – and loved me when I didn't deserve it, and He tells me to love others that way. How can I not be humble, broken, and nonjudgmental when that's what I've received from Him? It's a mandate as a Christian, not just for church planters who do outreach. If we would all reach out and love the way Jesus loves, we would all be a success story, because we will have learned the art of being a great Christian.

Staying Power

God's Assignment for You Right Now

by Fay Hedgepeth

On a cold, rainy Sunday morning in February 1964, John and I went to the first service at our first pastorate. The church was a conservative, rural church that had asked the conference superintendent for an educated pastor who didn't wear a "finger ring." After much prayer and discussion, John and I decided that he would take off his wedding band, since we felt God's leading in accepting this pastorate. My wearing a wedding band was not an issue.

After that first church service, we were greeting the 44 people present that day. Finally, the most influential woman of the church came up to me and asked, "Do you play the piano?"

"No."

Then she asked, "Do you play the organ?"

I answered, "No," while thinking, *If I can't play a piano, would I be able to play the organ?*

Finally, she asked a question with a tone in her voice that implied, I know you can do this: "You sing solos?"

Again, I had to answer, "No."

She responded, "We were hoping to get a pastor's wife who could do something."

That was my introduction into being a pastor's wife. Sometimes, the initiation into the sorority of pastors' wives is painful.

After staying at this church for almost 2½ years, we were assigned to another rural church. Vance Havner said that every minister should have to pastor a rural church. I tend to agree because lessons are learned there that you would find difficult to learn anywhere else.

Presently, we are at Northwood Temple in Fayetteville, North Carolina, our third pastorate. We have been here for 37 years. When we were assigned to Northwood in August 1968, we never dreamed we would stay in one place long enough to raise our children, see them married, and have our six grandchildren. As I reflect over our tenure at Northwood Temple, there are several factors that have contributed to our longevity.

Proper Mental Attitude

We have an evangelism ministry at Northwood Temple called "Evangelism Explosion," which was started by Dr. D. James Kennedy in Coral Ridge, Florida. As a part of the Evangelism Explosion program, witnessing teams go out each Tuesday night. Before they go, they join hands and pray for a divine appointment. When we were assigned to that first pastorate near Whiteville, North Carolina, we knew it was a divine appointment. Our second assignment in Princeton, North Carolina, was also a divine appointment. When we moved to Northwood Temple, we had the same assurance that it was another divine appointment. Proverbs 3:5-6 says, *"Trust in the Lord with all thine heart; and lean not unto thine own understanding. In all thy ways acknowledge him, and he shall direct thy paths."*

When your husband is given a ministry assignment, whether on the general, conference, or local level, it is important to accept it as a divine appointment. It's important to know that where you are serving right now is God's assignment for you at this present time. Sometimes, He gives us tough assignments, but it is in these tough places that we grow, mature, and become qualified for even greater service for our Lord. Never lose sight of why you are where you are.

Patsy Clairmont, author of *Normal Is Just a Setting on Your Dryer*, tells the story of being seated in an airplane by a young Marine returning from Desert Storm. In the conversation, she commented that he must have thought about returning to his family and home many times while he was in the Middle East. "Oh, no, ma'am," he replied, "we were taught never to think of what might never be, but to be *fully available* right where we are."

What great instruction – whether in the U.S. Marines or the Army of the Lord!

Paul, in his letter to the Philippians, the first church he founded on European soil, shared the circumstances of his imprisonment and rejoiced in his circumstances because they resulted in the spread of the gospel (1:12-26). Then in Philippians 4:11, he makes a profound statement: *"I have learned in whatever state I am, to be content"* (NKJV).

I have learned that wherever my husband is, I can be content and happy. Whatever state you're in right now – whether the best or the worst assignment – remember: this is God's assignment for you right now. Have the **proper mental attitude**.

> ***Prayer Point:*** *Holy Spirit, help me to accept God's assignment for me at this time, and to fulfill it with excellence and joy until He presents me with another.*

Partner With God

"Mission statement" is a buzzword today. Hospitals, schools, churches, department stores, businesses, clubs, organizations, etc., have mission statements for all to see. Jesus has given us a mission statement: *"Go therefore and make disciples of all the nations, baptizing them in the name of the Father and of the Son and the Holy Spirit, teaching them to observe all things that I have commanded you"* (Matthew 28:19, 20, NKJV).

"But you shall receive power when the Holy Spirit has come upon you; and you shall be witnesses to Me in Jerusalem, and in all Judea and Samaria, and to the end of the earth" (Acts 1:8, NKJV).

When we partner with God, we fulfill the Great Commission, His mission statement to us. We are on a mission for Jesus

Christ. Every organization, committee, and ministry of the church should have the common goal to witness and to make disciples of all men.

It is essential for this partnering to begin with the pastor. As the spiritual leader, the pastor must know God's assignment for his local church.

We were at Northwood four years before any growth took place. There were few salvations, and we were just another dead Pentecostal Holiness Church. We wanted our children to grow up in a church where they would experience God moving in a powerful way. It happened when John got down on his face before God in desperation and prayed, "God, give me souls, or take my life." That's when he partnered with God. That's when God's mission statement became his mission statement.

As a result, people were saved, sanctified, and filled with the Holy Spirit. The gifts of the Spirit were in operation. People were being healed. Other races and nationalities started coming, and we now have about 39 countries represented in our church. We strive for the ministries of the church to be based on winning souls and making disciples, whether it be through Sunday school, children's church, bus ministry, choir, drama, Women's Ministries, Men's Ministries, Evangelism Explosion, Bible studies, nursing homes, His Hands Extended, Mothers of Preschoolers (MOPS), Upward Basketball, Missions, thrift store, food pantry, or House of Hope Counseling Center ministering in the areas of chemical dependency, battered wives, nursing homes, etc.

It is important that the pastor's wife be a part of this partnering with God along with her husband. This has to be a team effort. If the pastor's wife is not committed to her husband's ministry, she will be a source of discouragement to him, and the congregation will sense that she is not a team player. For longevity in a pastorate, both the pastor and his wife must **partner with God**.

Love Your People

Jesus said in John 13:35, *"By this shall all men know that ye are my disciples, if ye have love one to another."* This powerful statement by our Lord is not just for the laity, but it includes both the pastor and his wife.

Even though we think of Paul as a great apostle, preacher, teacher, and missionary, he also had a pastor's heart of love. When he established a church, he didn't forget about it when he moved on to another city. He kept in touch with them by revisiting when possible, sending some of his helpers to check on them, and writing letters to them. To the Ephesians, he wrote, *"I do not cease to give thanks for you, making mention of you in my prayers"* (1:16, NKJV). To the Philippians he wrote, *"... I have you in my heart"* and *"... How greatly I long for you all with the affection of Jesus Christ"* (1:7, 8, NKJV). You can feel his love as you read the letters he wrote to the churches he established.

There is no substitute for love from the pastor and his wife. You can be a good preacher, teacher, administrator, organizer, and innovator, and you can have all the gifts of the Holy Spirit operating in you, but if you don't have love, you will not have a long, profitable ministry in one church. Just as a shepherd has love for his sheep, so must a pastor and his wife have love for their congregation. Because our congregation knows that we love them, they overlook many of our shortcomings. None of us is perfect in all our decisions and actions, but love covers a multitude of shortcomings.

This love will be reciprocal. When your congregation is convinced of your love, they will show their love to you in myriad ways. When we've experienced death in our family, our people have ministered to us with prayers, visits, flowers, food, even attending out-of-town funerals for our loved ones. When my mother was sick with cancer, our children were small. Several women in the church volunteered to keep them anytime I needed them. When she died, another woman washed and ironed our clothes while were out of town for the funeral. This woman had a full-time housekeeper who could have washed and ironed our clothes, but she chose to do them herself. It was a labor of love.

Another time, I fell down the stairs and injured my back. For two years, I was in bed more than I was up. The women of our church showed incredible love in their acts of service to our family during that time. When we have had family illnesses, they have shown their love for us, but they have also demonstrated their love with little acts of kindness for no reason at all. A church member who lives in our neighborhood walks early each morning. She brings our paper from the street down the hill to our house and lays it on our porch. We very seldom see her when she does this, but she does it faithfully.

It has not always been this way, however. When we came to Northwood Temple, the church was four years old, and John was their third pastor. Actually, some of the people wanted the previous pastor to stay. They were not happy that we were here. In fact, one lady would not speak to me for six months. It had nothing to do with me personally, because she didn't know me. She had just wanted the previous pastor to stay. We learned that there were two factions in the church. In fact, John said he felt like Pastor Salami sandwiched between two pieces of bread.

You might wonder what caused things to change. We had to build a relationship with them, and that takes time. With us, it took three or four years. We made a conscious effort to treat everyone the same. There could be no favoritism. It meant visiting, drinking a lot of coffee, complimenting, exhorting, and keeping a positive mental attitude when others were negative. It meant showing love to them in times of sickness, death, and family crises. It will not always be convenient to do so. Sickness and death have a habit of coming at inconvenient times. Once during those early years, we had just arrived at our vacation destination when we received a telephone call that someone in our church family had died. We explained to our children what had happened and that we would have to take our vacation later. We packed our bags and headed home. We didn't want our children to resent being PKs (Preacher's Kids). When things happened that changed our plans, we would explain to them that it was a part of their daddy's job, but we would also explain that other families sometimes had to change their plans because of their daddy's job. We would often use the military as an example. Living in a military community like Fort Bragg, we have learned that ministers' families are not the only ones who make such sacrifices. Military families make many sacrifices, especially when the father is deployed for months and years at a time.

During the early years of relationship building, we also built trust. As we were faithful to minister to them during their times of crises, they began to realize they could depend on us. We also built trust by not repeating things that were told to us in confidence. As professionals, we cannot afford to tell things of confidentiality.

We also let them know that not only did we love them, but we were also committed to them. We had no desire for the conference to assign us to a larger church. Our heart was to build Northwood into a larger church because we had a passion to win souls into the kingdom of God. We did not want to do it only through the transferring of memberships from other churches. We wanted to do it by winning people who were unchurched. This ties in with partnering with God and making God's mission statement our mission statement. The people bought into the vision, new ministries were started, and people were won into the kingdom of God.

> **Prayer Point:** *Seek God's help as you choose to love the people in your care. Pray for an increased capacity to receive love from those same people.*

Find Your Place of Ministry

The pastor's wife and children must find their places of ministry in the church. The pastor knows his place of ministry, but it is sometimes more difficult for his family, especially at the beginning of a new pastorate.

Sometimes a church has unrealistic expectations that a pastor's wife can do any job that the church can't find someone else to do. It's like the true story I shared at the beginning. Our first pastorate expected me to be a musician because they needed one. When I couldn't do that, they were disappointed. They didn't ask what I could do.

A pastor's wife is called on to wear many hats, but her fulfillment will not be in doing many things; it will come in serving in the place where God has gifted her. *"For as we have many members in one body, but all the members do not have the same function ... Having then gifts differing according to the grace that is given to us, let us use them ..."* (Romans 12:4, 6, NKJV).

One pastor's wife related that she had searched for years to discover her spiritual gift. When she took a spiritual gifts inventory, she realized she had the gift of exhortation. What a needed gift! In a world where so many things drag us down, exhorters come along to encourage us and give us a needed lift. This particular pastor's wife seemed to sense when a person needed a word of encouragement and was obedient in giving it. She failed to recognize it as a spiritual gift until she took a spiritual gifts inventory.

Sometimes a minister's wife mistakenly thinks she does not have a gift if she does not teach, sing, play an instrument, or do something before a group of people. That is not true! Some of the most vital gifts are the gifts of serving, mercy, and exhortation. Your part is to operate in the gift(s) God has given you. It would be unrealistic to think that a pastor's wife will not do things in the church outside her spiritual giftings. Out of necessity, you will have to do other things, but your sense of fulfillment will come from serving where God has gifted you.

Prayer Point: God, reveal to me the gifts you placed in my life. Even more, bless me with the creativity to use those gifts effectively in your kingdom.

It usually takes time in a new pastorate for the church to recognize the gifts of the pastor's wife. In each of the three churches we have pastored, it has taken time for me to serve as a teacher even though I seem to have the gift of teaching. Two things had to happen for me to use my spiritual gift. The church had to recognize my gift, and there had to be a vacancy. Through the years, I have taught young children, teens, young married couples, women's Bible studies, and adults. Each one has brought me a sense of fulfillment and satisfaction that no other job in the church has given me. If the pastor's wife is faithful and patient, God will open the door for her to serve according to the gift(s) He has given her.

Ministering in the same church for 37 years has been rewarding. Our children were able to grow up in one place. They have all gotten married and have had their children dedicated at Northwood Temple. Because of our long-term assignment, John has performed wedding ceremonies for couples, dedicated their children to the Lord, and has watched these children grow up into adults. Later, John has performed weddings for this second generation and dedicated their children to the Lord. We have ministered to families in joyful times during weddings, baby dedications, and graduations, and also during sorrowful times of sickness and death. We have gone full circle with some families from birth to death.

We have been able to be at Northwood Temple for 37 years because of a proper mental attitude, partnering with God, love for our congregation, and finding our place of ministry.

Give Me a Break

Ready to Retire ... Sort of

by Mary Burchett

When Rodney, our first-born, graduated from high school, we had no idea how hard it was going to be when he packed up his car and drove to Dallas ... alone ... to go to college. When Todd, our second-born, graduated from high school, he left for Tulsa to go to Oral Roberts University. That was easier. It was a lot closer, and surely we would get to see him more often then we did Rodney. With Shon, our youngest son, it was totally different. He enrolled in a local junior college and was still living at home. This was good. I was not ready to let Shon leave. He was going to stay home much longer.

About this time, Rodney had finished Christ for the Nations and also Fuller Theological Seminary in California, moved back to Oklahoma, and bought his own home. One Wednesday evening after service, the telephone rang. Dwight and I both picked up the phone, so I listened. It was Rodney, and he wanted to talk to Shon, who wasn't home, so Rodney asked his dad if he knew whether Shon was moving out this week or the next. Dwight said he didn't know.

I hung up the phone and panicked! I had a book about what to do when your nest is empty, but I hadn't read it yet. I shouldn't have been concerned because Shon was only moving in with his brother, and it was just down the street. Even so, when Shon came in, I went to his room and told him I heard he was moving out. "Please don't move out yet," I pleaded, "not until I find that book and read it, so I will know what to do when you leave."

He said, "Okay."

Well, let me tell you, I may have been dragged into the empty nest kicking and screaming, but that was not the case when we started to retire. I was ready, excited, and could hardly wait for the day to come. But, let me tell you the whole story.

In August 1962, six weeks before the birth of our first child, we attended the Oklahoma Pentecostal Holiness Camp Meeting. We had been evangelizing for a year, and I was ready to stop traveling, have my baby, and settle down to living in our own home.

Dwight was 20 years old, a little over six feet tall, and at that time weighed only 135 pounds. I was a little older, a lot shorter, and so big with child you could see me coming before I got there! What a sight we were, looking for a church to pastor.

Someone told us there would be a pastoral committee representative from Union Grove Church at camp meeting. We felt in our hearts that this was where God wanted us. We were told by friends and conference officials that Union Grove would be a good little church to start out with, and then when something better opened up in the city, we could "move on up." A few years later, our church became the largest in the conference.

The pastoral committee looked us over and took our phone number. The following weekend, we were asked to come and speak on the second Sunday of August. To this day, I feel sure we were asked to come and speak simply because we looked like we needed help. Their first project was to try to fatten up that poor preacher!

On that first Sunday, I remember driving to church, not really knowing where we were going. The road to Union Grove was not paved and was so far out in the woods that many evangelists who came to hold revivals said that even the Antichrist would not be able to find us out there! Right in the middle of the road was this sign with a big X on it that read, "You are here (X) because your husband won't stop and ask for directions." Yes, I am sure that is what it said. While we were stopped at that sign, a car passed us going south. Dwight said,

"They look like they may be going to church. Let's just follow them." And sure enough, we ended up at Union Grove Church.

After service that morning, we were invited to a member's home for dinner. What a spread they had on their table! We had never seen that much food for a dinner meal. It was like a holiday dinner, but that was their norm. Most of them were farmers, and they could put that food away. Dinner consisted of three meats, four vegetable dishes, three desserts, all kinds of salads, homemade bread, and all the trimmings. We were really in hog heaven!

After the Sunday evening service, they said, "Thanks for coming," and "It was nice to have you." Evidently, there must have been someone on the board who wasn't sure about having such a young couple as their pastor. Nevertheless, on Friday evening, we received another phone call and were asked to come and speak for the second time. We went, but still there was no word about becoming their pastor.

Finally, the following weekend, they asked us to come and be their pastor. We were thrilled. It took a couple of years of eating their cooking before Dwight started to put on some weight. Now, you might say he has become a "big preacher."

At the beginning of our pastorate, I felt overwhelmed at the many tasks a pastor's wife was expected to do. I had read many books written for pastors' wives. One particular book was entitled *Being a Pastor's Wife and Loving It*. I found out about being a pastor's wife, but didn't learn how to love it. I had many frustrations and questions.

It was while attending a Ministers' Wives Fellowship at a General Conference in Oklahoma City that I learned I was normal. What a relief that was! Thanks to Juanita Williams, our speaker, who somehow assured me I was sane after all. I soon took Philippians 4:11 to be my favorite scripture: "...For I have learned in whatsoever state [whether it be the state of Oklahoma, Texas, Hawaii, or Florida] I am, therewith to be content." My version is simply, "Grin and bear it." Believe me, I have held on to that scripture.

During those 40 years, I learned a pastor's wife needs to be "all things to all people." I wished many times for a PW (Pastor's Wife) degree of some sort, where I could be trained to be and do "all things." However, we learn through experiences, and each new experience causes us to grow. Those times of struggle are when you fall to your knees praying, "Help me, Lord, help me."

With each new position I took on, I found God's grace was sufficient for me. My favorite prayer became the traditional Irish prayer, "May those that love us, love us. And those that don't love us, may God turn their hearts. And if they won't turn their hearts, may they turn their ankles, so we'll know them by their limp. Amen."

We have many fond memories from those years, and a few we wish we could forget. But the best thing about pastoring was being where God wanted us and knowing we had a mission. Even so, I never dreamed it would be for 40 years. During our years of pastoring, God blessed our home with three sons, Rodney, Todd, and Shon, and our adopted daughter, Juliet. They, in turn, have blessed us with four beautiful granddaughters and four handsome grandsons.

At the church, we often had big days designed to help our church grow. One Easter Sunday, Dwight had three people dress in bright red devil costumes with horns and pitchfork tails. They were all on the front porch greeting people. You would be surprised how many church people were friendly with those devils! The devils tried to get the people to skip church, go back home, or go fishing at the lake a mile away. They even told some of them they had not seen them at church since last Easter and probably wouldn't see them again until next Easter. Now, Dwight could not have said those things! That was quite a day.

One Sunday evening, Dwight was preaching on the scripture, "Be not drunk with wine, wherein is excess; but be filled with the Spirit" (Ephesians 5:18). While we were singing, the door opened, and in walked a drunk man who staggered down the aisle, saying, "Brother Dwight. Where's Brother Dwight?" The congregation just sat there because they thought it was another one of the pastor's illustrated sermons. Dwight was seated behind a big podium and didn't hear the man come in. I was playing the organ and about to go into cardiac arrest because I knew it wasn't a skit. Finally, they got the man to the altar and prayed him through to salvation. He then sat on the front row and was the loudest "amen-er" Dwight has ever had in his lifetime. It was hilarious.

One night, we had a water baptism service, and the lady to be baptized was about as wide as she was tall. As Dwight was putting her under the water, she held her breath and floated. He struggled trying to get her baptized, but never did get her under the water. However, the congregation thought he was trying to drown the lady. This is one memory we will never forget.

For me, one of the hardest parts of the pastorate was to hear that someone – for some crazy, unknown, wrong, misunderstood reason – felt God had called them to leave the church. They then proceeded to uproot their family and replant them where something "new" was happening, or maybe to some church 30 miles across town. Sometimes, transplants do not live long. And sometimes they come back. Being at the same church for 40 years, we often got them back two or three times, maybe more. It seemed odd to me that God could not "make up His mind" where He wanted them to be planted. Now, if they are upset or disgruntled, let them go. We don't need that kind of attitude spreading through our churches. Pastoring would be so much more fun if it weren't for those kinds of people!

But praise the Lord for the faithful ones who stay with you no matter what happens, or no matter how many mistakes you may make. They stick with you through it all. We dearly love and appreciate those faithful members.

Once, when I was depressed and needed some attention from my busy, workaholic, pastor husband, I decided to write myself a letter and lay it on his desk. It read, "Dear Mary, my sweet darling honey. Thank you for being my wife. Thank you for being a wonderful part of my ministry. I appreciate all the help you give me and all the wonderful ideas you have. What would I do without you? I love you with all of my heart. I pray for you without ceasing. You are adorable and mine, only mine. Signed_____." And you know what? He signed it and gave it back to me with hugs and kisses. Men don't usually take hints very well, so you should just tell them what you need or write them a letter, if necessary, to get their attention.

The best thing about not being in the pastorate is the relief of stress. It is the most wonderful feeling to know it is no longer our responsibility. We don't have to sit on the front row any more. I get to sleep in on Sunday mornings and don't have to go to the early service. We don't have to dress up as much, but can dress more casually (so I've been delivered from panty hose). We don't have to stay until the last one leaves unless it is our turn to lock up. And if conflicts or troubles come, we can pray, but it is no longer our job to make the decisions or be in the middle of it. Praise the Lord! I get happier just thinking about it.

There are many more things I don't miss by not being in the pastorate. A big one is being told how I should dress, how much makeup I should wear, and how to fix my hair. For some reason, there are people who feel they own the pastor and his wife, and it is therefore their responsibility to tell them how to dress. As I said before, pastoring would be so much fun if it weren't for those kinds of people.

I'm sorry to say it, but along with retirement comes old age. Yes, if we live long enough, we will get old. And getting old is not fun. When did fun get to be so much work? Have you ever noticed that other people your age seem so much older than you? As I grow older, I find I need a lot of help. It takes me almost all day just to get ready. I put on my makeup (because I've heard if the barn needs painting, paint it!), decide what to wear (and that takes forever), fix my hair, pull in what needs to be pulled in, strap in things that might fall out, tuck my tummy into my pantyhose (and that takes work), put in my hearing aids and false teeth ... and by that time, it is almost bedtime. It won't be long until I will be up all night just getting ready for the next day!

About two years before we retired, I decided to go ahead and check out early (like early retirement), but I didn't tell anyone. It was my secret. I kept training others to do my job until I was free of church duties. I was ready to settle into my retirement and enjoy life. But then, my husband bought me a wedding chapel, thinking I needed something to do. Wrong! I worked harder at that chapel trying to help brides have the perfect wedding, and there is really no such thing, no matter how hard you practice!

God heard me yelling "Help!" again, and about two years later, I received a call from a lady looking for a church building. She asked if I would be interested in selling the chapel, and I said yes so fast my head was spinning. That was the easiest sale we ever made. Finally, I was ready to retire. I was saying, "Give me a break." I felt I had been there and done that. I wanted some time where I had nothing to do. I wanted to sleep in, shop, be lazy, rock in my rocker, read, or write a book. I love retirement.

When you retire, you need to make plans to prevent boredom from setting in. So far, I haven't had a boring day in my life. There is always something to do. But just in case, here are a few suggestions. Make sure you have a hobby. Now, Dwight's hobbies are (1) golf, (2) golf, and (3) more golf. My hobbies are (1) my eight grandkids, (2) shopping, and (3) the three Rs – reading, (w)riting, and riding in the RV. Other hobbies might consist of knitting (but don't get too carried away and knit a cover for the whole house!), crafts, volunteering, or exercise. Exercise is very important, but make it fun (exercise until it hurts, or for five minutes, whichever comes first). Try dancing. I used to be a dancer, but the music kept throwing me off!

When Shon was on staff with us for a few years, he was really growing in the Lord. We had always known in our hearts that God had His hand on him, and he was anointed for some ministry but not sure what that was to be. As time went on, he was being mentored for the pastorate. For a few months, he and

Dwight copastored, and in August 2002, the mantle was passed on to Shon from his dad, and Shon became our pastor. The church gave Dwight a retirement party, but he told everyone he was not retiring, just retiring. He stayed on staff and is over the OASIS (Older Adults Still in Service), the Missions Department, and the POS leaders (Positively Outrageous Service). He loves his job, and he does not want to quit ... ever.

Since retiring, Dwight has been asked many times if he misses pastoring, and his answer is always negative. He still loves to preach, but he decided it was time to pass the pastoring duties on when they quit being fun. His present job does not compare to a full-time pastorate, and he will probably stay there forever.

> **Prayer Point:** *Heavenly Father, help me to understand and believe that retirement does not mean our ministry is finished. Retirement from the employ of the church simply means we're on staff for you ... full time.*

We were created to have fellowship with God. Our life here on earth is such a short span compared to eternity. We are in training to live forever. Every day we live should be for the glory of God. He should be included in all our activities.

We may be the only Bible some people read. May God help us not be a hindrance to those who are in darkness. The world lives in darkness, and our light should shine to show them there is a better life. In Ecclesiastes 3, there are a lot of times to do this and do that, but it does not mention a time to retire. Am I retired? Yes, from the position of being the lead pastor's wife, but not from doing what God has asked me to do. God still uses us and has a plan for us even though we are no longer in the limelight. As long as we are breathing, we will and can accomplish what God has for us to do. There is something we can do for His kingdom wherever we go.

P.S. Do you really want to know the one thing I miss the most since not being the lead pastor's wife? We had our own private restroom connected to the pastor's office. And you know what? Now I have to go to the big one. What a bummer!

My Guided Life

"God, please don't forget we are here!"

by Faye Leggett

On a recent Sunday afternoon, I was going through some old books when I came across a diary from my days as a student at Holmes Bible College. I spent most of the afternoon reading and reliving the events of 1959. It brought back memories of a 17-year-old girl at college, and of the wonderful experiences that shaped her life.

The most important date that year was May 29, 1959. That was the day a young man named James Leggett asked me to be his wife. We were married two years later, June 25, 1961, in my home church, Lens Avenue (Parkway Temple) Pentecostal Holiness Church. I remember clearly when James said he wanted us "to do the will of God and for me to make him happy." That day, I knew I was going to be a minister's wife. My husband's requests became my standard. We started a journey together to serve the Lord in ministry, always seeking to know and do His will.

The first year of our marriage and our ministry was spent at Holmes Bible College, where James taught. It was a happy year, full of discovery, and we enjoyed the time together. Although he taught at Holmes only one year, he has always enjoyed teaching and later taught extension classes in North Carolina for Holmes and Emmanuel.

As the school year came to a close, James felt that it was time ... he had to pastor. We began to pray and seek God's direction. James informed Rev. W. Eddie Morris that he would like to be considered for an appointment at the upcoming

Quadrennial Conference. Yes, that was in the day when the superintendent made the appointments, and you found out on Sunday night where you were going. Thank the Lord, that has changed.

As pastors' wives, we all had dreams when our husbands asked us to marry, dreams of how ministry together would be. Those dreams continue to be tested by reality, for things are not always like we dreamed. Yet, with all of its surprises and changes, pastoring is one of the most joyful and fulfilling lives. After almost 50 years of ministry, I can still rejoice in the wonderful life that God has given to us.

Our first assignment was a two-church charge: Swanquarter and Pinetown, in coastal North Carolina. We lived in Swanquarter, and Pinetown was 40 miles away. One Sunday, we preached at Swanquarter, and the next Sunday, we drove to Pinetown and spent the entire day, returning after the Sunday night service.

Now, truthfully, I was a city girl raised in Norfolk, Virginia, and I had spent the last six years of my life in Greenville, South Carolina. When I arrived in Swanquarter, a small fishing village, it was culture shock. We were 30 miles from the nearest town, and even it was small. The only town of size was nearly 60 miles away. I remember going outside that first night and looking up at the sky. "Lord," I prayed, "you see me here, and I know I have prayed for the will of God to guide our lives, so please don't forget that we're here."

We pastored there for two years. I substituted for the piano player, but could only play three or four songs. I guess everyone in the congregation learned those three songs so well they could sing them by memory. They could probably predict each Sunday which one I was going to play.

When our two-year appointment was complete, James asked to be moved. The conference board, without consulting us, sent us back to Swanquarter ... without the Pinetown appointment. My husband traveled to Falcon and tried to impress on the superintendent that he felt it was time to relocate. After a few more months, the superintendent called us with an appointment to Pembroke. This turned out to be a very providential move. I have heard my husband refer to this move frequently as a clear statement of God's direction for our lives. Suppose we had acted in frustration and left Swanquarter when the conference did not move us. We would have missed a major step in God's direction for our lives. If we are to follow God's direction and stay in His will, we must learn to deal with roadblocks, dead ends, and frustrations. We need to look and see what God is doing. He may have something wonderful in store for us. He certainly did for our lives in Pembroke. God knew far better than we did, and Pembroke was a divine appointment on the path of our lives in the work of the kingdom.

Pembroke was a college town, and the church was across the street from the college. The church had one of the largest Sunday schools in the conference at that time. We came from a church where we had 15 to 30 on a given Sunday. Pembroke had over 200 most Sundays.

Mrs. Oxendine approached James soon after our arrival, encouraged him to attend Pembroke College (now University of North Carolina at Pembroke), and promised to pay all his tuition. James waited until he built a new educational building for the church and then enrolled. Though Edna Lee died before he graduated, her husband, Mr. Hubert Oxendine, paid the tuition. The Lord knew the future He had for my husband and guided him to Pembroke by divine appointment.

We spent six years at the Mount Olive Church in Pembroke. We were happy there, but the Lord began stirring our hearts again. We prayed and sought God, wanting above all His will for our lives. This was a very difficult time for me. I loved the people at the church and hated to leave them. I was comfortable where I was. I did not want to move. I did not like change.

When James came home from conference and told me that we were assigned to pastor the Culbreth Memorial Church in Falcon, it was the one place I did not want to go. Culbreth was a unique church because of its location at the conference campground and headquarters. I was concerned that I would not fit there. I wasn't sure I was qualified for such a church. I looked at my shortcomings and feared I would never measure up to the expectations. Nor did I look forward to living in the fishbowl of the conference leadership. But once again, the Lord had a plan, and that plan was in motion. He knew where He was leading. He knew what was best for our lives. Looking back now, I can easily trace His hand in all the changes of our lives.

While my husband was at the camp meeting one night, I sought the Lord with tears and supplications. I was broken before Him. That night, God spoke to me so clearly, I could not doubt. He whispered into my spirit, "This is my appointment for you, and James will not leave Falcon to pastor another church." When my husband came home, he was surprised at the change in my attitude. I shared with him what the time of prayer brought forth and the message God spoke to my heart. I think he had some doubts. Neither of us shared this with anyone until after we left the pastorate in Pembroke. I learned once again, and this time with deeper conviction, that when I really commit my life to God, He is faithful to guide and lead each step of the way.

> ***Prayer Point:*** *God, teach me to bring my concerns to you in prayer. The turmoil within often becomes unbearable, but you can calm the waters with a word to my heart.*

The 16 years as a pastor's wife in Falcon were a good training ground. I learned so much from the women of the church and the association with conference leadership. It was truly preparation for the future work to which God called my husband.

As a pastor's wife, I learned what was most important in my life and ministry. My priorities in life and ministry are God first, then my husband and my children, and then ministry. My first calling is to be sure I am in the center of God's will for my life and then to take care of my family: my husband and children.

It is my responsibility to provide a home for them that is a haven and a place of rest. My children were the priority. They were given to me by God as a sacred trust. They were not to be neglected while I was busy doing church work.

Looking back over our years in the pastorate, I can see how God was preparing both of us for the future in denominational leadership. During our pastorate in Falcon, I was elected to serve as president of Women's Ministries for the North Carolina Conference. It was a position I had not sought and did not really want. Once again, I questioned my qualification for such a responsibility. Even as I questioned, I was reassured that this was God's plan and place for my life. I went to Mrs. Luetta Morris and poured out my heart with all the concerns about serving in this capacity, especially while being a pastor's wife and the mother of four children. She gave me words of wisdom that day. She told me, "If God wants you to serve as WM president, He will give you strength and wisdom to do both and to make your children a part of the work." How true her words were! Cindy, my daughter, traveled with me from church to church, and my son John helped me stuff packets for meetings. Cindy even told her father, "I can preach mother's sermons, I've heard them so many times." Despite my earlier misgivings, it was a joy and privilege to work with the great ladies of the conference. It was during this time I was elected to the General Women's Ministries Board.

As we were finishing 16 years of pastoring the Falcon church, the winds of change began to blow. I knew that, once again, I had to prepare for change and, once again, it would be difficult. We had such a good pastorate, and the people were like family to us and to our children. Yet James and I both knew that the direction of our lives was about to change. I remembered the words God spoke to me 16 years earlier and trusted Him for our future.

Prayer Point: Ask God to prepare your heart for change. Be willing for the Potter to shape you on His wheel, for His purposes.

147

James was elected superintendent of the North Carolina Conference in the summer of 1986. This was not nearly as traumatic as moving to another pastorate, for we would continue to live in Falcon, and we would finally get to live in our own home. I will never forget the feeling of having my very own home – not a parsonage. Every pastor's wife ought to have that joy.

There was a big change, though. I had thoroughly enjoyed being a pastor's wife. They were great years, and I still miss serving alongside my husband in the pastorate. It is truly one of the greatest places of service in the kingdom.

As the superintendent's wife, I became the Ministers' Wives director for the conference. It was during this time that I began to feel a burden and love for the ministers' wives. Through our ministry there, I understand more than ever the needs, hurts, and wounds of these special women, as well as their joys. When we had our first Ministers and Wives retreat in Greenville, North Carolina, women wrote us notes of thanks and asked for more attention to their needs. Some of the notes were unsigned because the women expressed the desperation they were experiencing in trying to cope with their situations.

Though I still missed the pastorate greatly, I soon found myself enjoying ministry in the conference. It was great to get up on Sunday morning and travel with my husband across the conference, preaching at the different churches. In fact, Sunday mornings became a special time for us. We could spend the time together, talking and sharing without interruptions. There were no cell phones to bring problems, and we could have quality time together. Sometimes now, when we travel locally on a Sunday, the trip across Oklahoma will bring back fond memories of those days.

As superintendent's wife, I still endeavored to live by the priorities I established as pastor's wife: God first, my husband and my family, ministry to ministers' wives and the people of the conference.

Our time as superintendent was short ... too short. After only three years as conference superintendent, James was elected as one of the assistant general superintendents of the IPHC with the portfolio of Evangelism (EVUSA). Even though in my heart I knew it was going to happen, it was the most difficult change in my life. I had lived in Falcon now for 19 years, longer than any other place in my life. I was very comfortable. This move would certainly take me out of my comfort zone. This time, I would be leaving my children and my first grandchild. The turmoil in my heart was such that I suggested to my husband he decline the appointment so we could return to Falcon.

I don't think I will ever forget, though time has soothed the pain, when I hugged my children and my granddaughter goodbye and headed to Oklahoma. I can cry even now when I think of that day.

Soon, I became adjusted to living in Oklahoma, but there was a problem. For the first time in my husband's ministry, I did not seem to have a place to serve. In the pastorate, I had been involved in Girls' Ministries, teaching Sunday school, and Women's Ministries, but now there was no avenue for me to minister. James was on the road most weekends, and I was at home. Even as wife of the superintendent, I had been involved in conference work, visiting churches, and directing Minister's Wives Fellowship. Now, there was nothing. It took a long time to adjust to this lack of contact in ministry. It was almost like an empty place in my heart.

One more change was on the horizon. It would not be relocation, but a change of position. In 1997, James was elected as general superintendent of our denomination, replacing Bishop Underwood, who retired. I was extremely proud of my husband, and I knew this was the will of God our lives and the IPHC. The morning after the election, I remained in my hotel room to fall on my face before the Lord, asking Him to help me understand where my place was. I wanted to know if I would have to change who I am. "I have always tried to be real and to be me. Do I have to change to meet others expectations?" As I cried, my wonderful, beautiful Savior seemed to whisper to me, "I have chosen you like you are." I felt a burden leave me that morning. As long as God is pleased with me, and my husband is happy with me, then I can always be real and be me.

> ***Prayer Point:*** *Thank God for His unconditional love for you. Thank Him that His plan and purpose for your life were created for the person you are.*

As wife of the general superintendent, I was appointed director of Ministers' Wives Fellowship for the church. This enabled me once more to work with pastors' wives, this time across our denomination. I thank God that I have been allowed to be a part of the church today and to see firsthand what great and mighty things He is doing in the world. It is a joy to visit churches all over the U.S.A. and around the world, and to witness the move of God in the IPHC. I am thankful for the privilege of meeting and working with such wonderful people in this denomination.

What a wonderful journey this has been! I can trace the hand of God in all the many changes. He has been my constant guide. From the time I was a little girl in the old Lens Avenue Church in Norfolk, my life has been guided by the Lord. He has given me wonderful opportunities to serve as the wife of a pastor and as a partner in ministry. Who would ever have thought, when I was a high school student at Holmes, that I would have the privilege to serve in leadership in the Pentecostal Holiness Church? God thought it, and God brought it to pass.